Florida A&M University, Tallahassee
Florida Atlantic University, Boca Raton
Florida Gulf Coast University, Ft. Myers
Florida International University, Miami
Florida State University, Tallahassee
University of Central Florida, Orlando
University of Florida, Gainesville
University of North Florida, Jacksonville
University of South Florida, Tampa
University of West Florida, Pensacola

Also by Michael Patrick Gillespie, from the University Press of Florida

Oscar Wilde and the Poetics of Ambiguity (1996)

Joyce through the Ages: A Nonlinear View (1999)

University Press of Florida

Gainesville Tallahassee Tampa Boca Raton

Pensacola Orlando Miami Jacksonville Ft. Myers

The Aesthetics of

Chaos

Nonlinear Thinking and Contemporary Literary Criticism

Michael Patrick Gillespie

08 07 06 05 04 03   6 5 4 3 2 1

Library of Congress Cataloging-in-Publication Data
Gillespie, Michael Patrick
The aesthetics of chaos: nonlinear thinking and contemporary
literary criticism / Michael Patrick Gillespie.
p. cm.
Includes bibliographical references and index.
ISBN 0-8130-2641-5 (cloth: alk. paper)
1. Criticism—History—20th century.
PN94.A33 2003
801'.95'0904—dc21 2003040239

The University Press of Florida is the scholarly publishing
agency for the State University System of Florida, comprising
Florida A&M University, Florida Atlantic University, Florida
Gulf Coast University, Florida International University,
Florida State University, University of Central Florida,
University of Florida, University of North Florida, University
of South Florida, and University of West Florida.

University Press of Florida
15 Northwest 15th Street
Gainesville, FL 32611–2079
http://www.upf.com

To Chuck and Linda Yung

Contents

Acknowledgments

I have always found this to be the most difficult section of a book to write. I am afraid that any effort to thank the people who offered advice, insight, or support from which I benefited while working on this study will come far short of the acknowledgment that each deserves. I will not belabor the contributions of each, but I hope in the alphabetical listing that follows that I can attest to their generosity of spirit. With this in mind, I would like to express my gratitude to the following: Jonathan Allison, Zack Bowen, Mary Elizabeth Braun, the Rev. Thaddeus Burch, S.J., William Demastes, Deirdre Dempsey, A. Nicholas Fargnoli, Susan Fernandez, Anne Fogarty, Paula Gillespie, Judy Goffman, Amy Gorelick, Cheryl Herr, Philip Herring, Debra Jelacic, Morton Levitt, Tim Machan, Peter Mackey, Michael McKinney, Valerie Murrenus, Sandra Peterson, John Rickard, Thomas Rice, Gary Richardson, Albert Rivero, Thomas Shea, Robert Spoo, John Su, the Rev. Roland Teske, S.J., George Watson, and Stephen Watt. Whatever weaknesses one may find in this work, there are far fewer because of the help I received from these friends.

An earlier version of chapter 3 appeared as an article in the *Journal of Modern Literature*. I am grateful to Indiana University Press for permission to reprint it here.

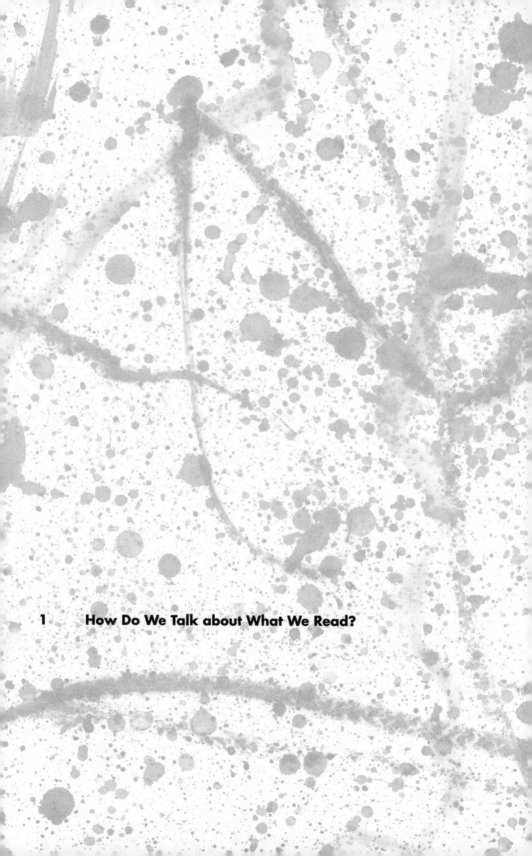

1   How Do We Talk about What We Read?

NEARLY A CENTURY AGO, at about the same time that Ferdinand de Saussure was introducing a revolutionary approach to linguistics, and long before Saussure's ideas were published, James Joyce was demonstrating the difficulties that individuals from different backgrounds encounter in their efforts to derive meaning from a language that each claims as his own. The well-known exchange, in chapter 5 of *A Portrait of the Artist as a Young Man*, between Stephen Dedalus and the dean of students over their conceptions of the words *funnel* and *tundish* nicely illustrates the confusion that grows out of the assumption that words have an essential rather than an indefinite or even an arbitrary quality:

> —To return to the lamp, [the dean] said, the feeding of it is also a nice problem. You must choose the pure oil and you must be careful when you pour it in not to overflow it, not to pour in more than the funnel can hold.
> —What funnel? asked Stephen.
> —The funnel through which you pour the oil into your lamp.
> —That? said Stephen. Is that called a funnel? Is it not a tundish?
> —What is a tundish?
> —That. The . . . funnel.
> —Is that called a tundish in Ireland? asked the dean. I never heard the word in my life.
> —It is called a tundish in Lower Drumcondra, said Stephen laughing, where they speak the best English.[1]

As Stephen and perhaps the dean discover over the course of their exchange, the sense of stability that both men initially presume to exist in language proves to be little more than a habituation to the approximate way by which words convey intended meaning.

A cursory examination of contemporary literary studies seems to indicate a near universal awareness of this ambiguity. Any number of critics readily acknowledge in a general fashion the linguistic slipperiness illustrated by the passage quoted above. They endorse the idea that the meaning that we attach to words comes out of a multilayered consciousness made up of expectations, recollections, associations, and sensations exerting varying force from one exchange to the next. And these critics quite often go on to assert that understanding grows out of personal experience, contextualized in a specific culture, tempered by education, shaped by attentiveness, and warped by one's prevailing disposition at the time—which has a profound effect upon how any of us might understand a collection of words gathered into phrases, sentences, and paragraphs. Nonetheless, when some individuals make specific responses to particular works, they still follow the same pattern of objectifying, exclusionary, cause-and-effect logic in examinations·

of literature that we encounter in literary commentaries ranging back as far as Aristotle's *Poetics*.[2]

The narrow and inexorably linear form of analysis at the heart of literary criticism proceeds out of the belief that reading should produce a unified response to the words on the printed page.[3] No matter what thematic or ideological assumptions inform the activity, the search for cause-and-effect relationships, made familiar through the widespread acceptance of Newtonian thinking, continues to dominate current interpretive methods. This concept gives the derivation of meaning a symbiotic momentum. One idea or observation creates facts that serve as the basis for deriving subsequent ideas or observations. As each view generates successive perspectives, the range of inquiry narrows progressively until a single, unified comprehension emerges.

Unfortunately, even the best critics find themselves unconsciously bound to this approach, which produces interpretations far too narrow to accommodate the full potential of literary expression. Let me illustrate my point by contrasting two reactions to the opening sentences of *Ulysses*:

> Stately, plump Buck Mulligan came from the stairhead, bearing a bowl of lather on which a mirror and a razor lay crossed. A yellow dressinggown, ungirdled, was sustained gently behind him on the mild morning air. He held the bowl aloft and intoned:
>
> —*Introibo ad altare Dei*.[4]

Bernard Benstock, one of the most respected Joyce scholars of his generation, provides a representative example of how a reader might deal with those lines by following the conventional mode of Cartesian analysis, in this case isolating distinctive characteristics of what he sees as the narrative voice: "'Stately, plump Buck Mulligan' as a descriptive phrase has a dignity-cum-pomposity befitting the Buck and might well be his own self-descriptiveness at work. In these opening moments, while Mulligan remains alone, narrative tone is maintained close to the character. . . ."[5] With the consummate skill of a critic trained in the process of highlighting a specific aspect of the reading experience, Benstock demonstrates his considerable interpretive abilities. In two brief sentences, he characterizes the description of Mulligan in a fashion that shows a deft sense of the nuances of language. Nonetheless, the rigidity of linear conventions limits Benstock's options for exploiting linguistic diversity to observations that relate solely to a central idea. When we compare his statement to the impressions that arise from an ordinary reading of the passage, we see that this formal interpretive assessment represents a greatly truncated version of the reaction that we might normally expect a reader, not inhibited by the protocols of Cartesian interpretation, to make.

To me, for example, these opening lines provoke complex and unstable imaginative responses almost always involving a series of diverse and highly personal associations tempered by literary, historic, and cultural experiences. The first two words describing Mulligan—"Stately, plump"—may lead me to conjure a picture of him as a younger version of former Senator Daniel Patrick Moynihan. The narrative's setting recalls for me impressions from the visits that I have made to the cramped confines of the top of the Martello Tower in Sandycove, in which Joyce and Oliver St. John Gogarty lived for a short time in 1904. The Latin phrase *Introibo ad altare Dei* ("I will go unto the altar of God") may elide my picture of Mulligan as Senator Moynihan with an image of Father William Dorney, longtime priest at my neighborhood parish, standing at the altar on numerous early mornings in St. Angela's Church on the west side of Chicago, saying Mass at a time when Latin was still the language of worship. And I will inevitably play all of these impressions against my evolving conception of the fictional events in the narrative, shaped and reshaped by numerous previous readings.

Further, the subjectivity of this response is matched by its impermanence. Whenever I open *Ulysses*, a dozen other and very different associations, all relevant to me at the moment of reading, may stream through my consciousness and shape my impressions of the words on the page. The point is, in this instance and in numerous other examples that I could adduce, my reading resists the linear patterning inherent in the work of the traditional critic. This fundamental difference between the cognitive process followed by a reader and the hermeneutic methods followed by a critic challenges the relevance of traditional interpretive commentary. In contrast to the complex associations of any individual's impressions, current forms of analysis inevitably produce reductive views. Consequently, if critics hope to discuss literature with the same depth that ordinary readers experience it, a new approach, one that articulates the multiplicity of the occasion, is needed.

To some, this imperative to discern the diversity inherent in the experience of reading literature will sound achingly familiar, a reprise of the condition that animates any of a number of approaches that insist upon the indeterminacy of meaning. Certainly, acknowledging pluralism is an important step in understanding the interpretive process. In fact, as I have already noted, the idea of multiplicity has itself become a critical commonplace. Unfortunately, despite the ambitious aims for inclusiveness and diversity expressed by many contemporary interpretive approaches, they by and large remain tied to a linear system of analysis that ensures that some measure of exclusion will always inform their conclusions. Indeed, no matter what jargon is invoked to occlude the process, cause-and-effect thinking has insistently dominated interpretive perceptions for nearly four centuries through its methodical ability to eliminate alternatives in order to arrive at a definitive point of view.

Literary critics have become so inured to the inevitable inconsistencies of this approach that as a reflex action they simply ignore particulars that do not fit the narrow assumptions that unify their criticisms. Newtonian scientists, encountering similar irregularities in their experiments, dismiss these elements as "white noise." In this fashion, they deftly sidestep anomalies that resist the regularizing efforts of cause-and-effect logic, and at times overlook important data that fall outside their analytical paradigm.[6] Most literary critics do not even make this overt concession. Anomalous details become invisible because they do not appear within the point of view prescribed by the reader's approach.

The dominance of metaphors shaped by Newtonian perceptions of the world has inhibited the development of approaches that capture the diversity of a reader's encounter with literature. For example, in talking about literature, an individual might describe the process as "focusing on a central idea, weighing the evidence, and balancing opposing views to arrive at a conclusion." With the advent of post-Einsteinian physics, a new language for describing the world has evolved, and that now stands as a ready lexicon for more complete descriptions of the interpretive process. (I will elaborate on that language in the next chapter.) However, before laying out my alternative to cause-and-effect thinking, I wish to clarify the differences between this method and others by summarizing previous efforts of literary critics to move to a different paradigm and noting how a dependence upon linearity has ensured the failure of these efforts. What follows is intended as a representative sampling rather than an exhaustive survey. My aim here is simply to show the way cause-and-effect logic blunts the possibilities of even the most creative interpretive approaches.[7]

In the appendix, I trace the steps by which, as early as the late nineteenth century, physicists and mathematicians were advancing scientific theories based upon analytical assumptions that would undermine the primacy of linear thinking. At roughly the same time, literary critics were engaged in parallel endeavors in aesthetic theory, seeking to escape the restraints of Cartesian logic. Walter Pater's groundbreaking 1873 book, *Studies in the History of the Renaissance*, stands as most noteworthy for both its critical and social implications. Although his views may seem tame, even conservative, to contemporary readers, the concept that Pater forwarded, that art defines itself through its beauty and not through its moral or utilitarian functions, directly challenged modes of interpretation championed by critics like John Ruskin and insinuated, without elaboration, a kind of subjectivity in meaning that cause-and-effect logic would not tolerate.

Pater, however, remained a cautious proponent of this new way of describing what we see in art. He left to disciples, like Oscar Wilde, the task of pushing this valuation of beauty to the point of disrupting conventional modes of critical thinking. Though *Punch* lampooned him as an "art for art's sake" aesthete, Wilde articulated aesthetic views that went well beyond such a glib categorization. His most ambitious critical efforts appear in the essays collected in the volume *Intentions*, and they include a direct assault upon objectivist critical assumptions ("The Decay of Lying"), a sharp distinction between aesthetic and moral judgments ("Pen, Pencil and Poison"), and a celebration of the imagination over factual accuracy ("The Picture of Mr. W.H.").[8] However, his efforts and those of Arthur Symons, who endeavored to expand upon Pater's approach in *The Symbolist Movement in Literature* and elsewhere, lacked the organization (and in Wilde's case perhaps the gravitas) necessary to gain support in academic circles, and despite their initial popularity both men came to be dismissed as idiosyncratic.

By the 1920s, with the revolution in modern physics well under way, critical thinking in literature had if anything taken a retrograde turn by re-emphasizing the importance of the certitude provided by a Cartesian worldview. In the essay "Tradition and Individual Talent," published in *The Sacred Wood* in 1920, T. S. Eliot enshrines the linearity of literature by his celebration of an accretive approach to creativity. Stating that a poet makes his own tradition by using the materials of the past, Eliot stamps literature with an evolutionary mold that features linearity as a key feature in the comprehension of the artistic process. Through Eliot's recuperative approach, the diverse allusions of a poem like *The Waste Land*, widely proclaimed as a paragon of Modernist writing, in fact demonstrate the work's linear development out of the past as it gains unity and direction from an overarching artistic tradition.

More overt affinity for conventional scientific approaches influenced other literary thinkers. The most direct connection appeared in the work of I. A. Richards. Early on, in *The Meaning of Meaning* (coauthored in 1923 with C. K. Ogden), Richards offers pioneering linguistic insights on the role of the imagination in the creation of meaning. His 1924 book, *The Principles of Literary Criticism*, presents more specific guidelines for reading. Seeing poems as complex structures highly dependent upon context, Richards asserts that criticism necessarily elaborates upon the condensed language of the poem. In *Practical Criticism* (1929), Richards articulates an approach to interpretation founded upon the investigative principles informed by Newtonian science. In this book Richards describes an experiment in which he asked students to examine poems stripped of all extratextual information (and even information some would consider intratextual, such as the author and date of composition). Through this combination of linguistic sophistication and conventional scientific analysis, Richards' work legitimized Cartesian principles of literary interpretation and laid the groundwork in England for a mode of assessment that would dominate critical thinking in Great Britain and North America for decades to come.

From the late 1920s in America, a similar form of interpretive analysis based on the use of close reading to formalize the qualities of poetic thought and language was gaining popularity, especially among a group of Southern writers and critics—including Allen Tate, John Crowe Ransom, and Robert Penn Warren—associated with the Agrarian movement. In 1941 Ransom gave a name to that approach when he published *The New Criticism*. Doubtless this work clarified the methodology, and the ensuing popularity of the New Critical approach regularized the steps followed in conventional searches for meaning. At the same time, despite its widespread appeal, New Criticism did little to accommodate the flexibility of the individual reader, and instead forwarded a prescriptive approach to discerning meaning.

Of course, even while the views of Richards and the New Critics were gaining esteem, alternatives to these approaches also enjoyed popular support. F. R. Leavis in particular emerged as a formidable and influential voice on reading literature, at least in Great Britain. The interpretive programs that he laid out for poetry in *New Bearings in English Poetry* (1932) and *Revaluation: Tradition and Development in English Poetry* (1936) and for fiction in *The Great Tradition* (1948), as well as the ideas that he cultivated as editor of the literary journal *Scrutiny* (1932–53), effectively set the mold for criticism until well into the 1970s.

Leavis' work stands in a unique relation to that of contemporaries like Richards and William Empson (*The Seven Types of Ambiguity*, 1930). Like most approaches of the time, Leavis' ideas show a profound respect for the work itself: "In dealing with individual poets the rule of the critics is, or should (I think) be, to work as much as possible in terms of particular analysis—analysis of poems or passages, and to say nothing that cannot be related immediately to judgments about producible texts."[9] At the same time, an aggressive extratextuality surrounds his readings. He sees literature as intimately related to life, and he calls upon the critic to assess the writer's moral position especially with regard to the concept of tradition: "[W]e may say that the less important poets bear to tradition an illustrative relation, and the more important bear to it the more interesting kinds of relation: they represent significant development."[10]

The passages just quoted underscore the central problem in Leavis' approach: the conflicted nature of the views that he sought to impose upon the reader. On the one hand, his methods confer a great deal of freedom on the acts of perception and judgment. At the same time, as he reminds the reader, a hierarchical structure of greater and lesser also plays an important part in every interpretive act. Indeed, within the orderly Cartesian world that characterizes Leavis' analytical thinking, conditions could hardly be otherwise. However, this adherence to conventional modes is precisely what threatens the effectiveness of those efforts by binding each with prescriptive limitations.

During the period in which Leavis was writing, Mikhail Bakhtin was developing radically different ways of talking about literature (though his ideas did not become available to Western critics until much later). In his emphasis on the dialogic, Bakhtin's analysis foregrounds the social context of interpretation, functioning under the designation *heteroglossia*. In the following passage from perhaps his best-known work, *The Dialogic Imagination*, Bakhtin succinctly explains how heteroglossia works in the novel: "as a diversity of social speech types (sometimes even diversity of languages) and a diversity of individual voices, artistically organized. . . . Authorial speech, the speeches of narrators, inserted genres, the speech of characters are merely those fundamental compositional unities with whose help heteroglossia can enter the novel; each of them permits a multiplicity of social voices and a wide variety of their links and interrelationships (always more or less dialogized)."[11]

These views, especially when compared with contemporary thinking, stand out as refreshingly open-minded. Nonetheless, Bakhtin does not find limitless interpretation in the diversity that he perceives. Rather, while he argues that the reader's recognition of such competing demands leads to a greatly expanded hermeneutic perception, the dialogism so important to his interpretive responses remains Cartesian and hierarchical: "Heteroglossia, once incorporated into the novel (whatever the forms for its incorporation), is *another's speech in another's language*, serving to express authorial intentions but in a refracted way. Such speech constitutes a special type of *double-voiced discourse*. It serves two speakers at the same time and expresses simultaneously two different intentions: the direct intention of the character who is speaking, and the refracted intention of the author" (emphasis Bakhtin's).[12] Bakhtin's discourses occur on different levels, and they function with a weighted (and in my view seriously misplaced) significance ascribed to authorial intentionality.

As with other twentieth-century literary theorists, Bakhtin showed an admirable resistance to a single level of reading. At the same time, also like many of his contemporaries, Bakhtin needed an anchor to hold his hypotheses in place. He fell back on the polarities of either/or thinking and upon the hierarchies of privileged meanings. While his ideas did much to open up approaches to narrative interpretation, they could not escape the limitations imposed by linearity.

Western critics would not have the benefits of Bakhtin's insights for decades, and the shifting intellectual climate following the conclusion of World War II produced a great deal of restiveness and concomitant efforts to find certitude in critical methods. In 1957, in what became for many of that era the preeminent codification of interpretive thought, Northrop Frye published *Anatomy of Criticism*. While any number of the ideas that Frye propounded may be dismissed as quaint by anyone nurtured on the views of the French philosophers of the 1960s, Frye's book nonetheless stands out as one of the most influential critical works to appear before the wave of Deconstructionism would challenge the legitimacy of such formal conceptions of literature.

In *Anatomy of Criticism* Frye endeavors to outline what he sees as an "intermediary system" serving as a buffer between the prejudicial reaction of personal taste and the proscriptive inhibition of an imposed system. Frye's writing vehemently challenges the efficacy of the individuality advocated by those who distorted the views of Pater and Wilde: "A public that tries to do without criticism, and asserts that it knows what it wants or likes, brutalizes the arts and loses its cultural memory."[13] At the same time, Frye has very strict ideas regarding what constitutes a valid critical methodology. He opposes what he calls "determinisms in criticism," guilty of "substituting a critical attitude for criticism, all proposing, not to find a conceptual framework for criticism within literature, but to attach criticism to one of a miscellany of frameworks outside it."[14]

These are not the sentiments of a curmudgeon. In his "Polemical Introduction" and throughout *Anatomy of Criticism*, Frye's passion for literature could not be more evident. Likewise, I find admirable his desire to present mediation between positions that he perceives as critical extremes. In the end, however, an exclusionary linearity permeates the arguments of *Anatomy of Criticism* and frustrates these endeavors. The critical approaches represented in his four essays form a single system held in equilibrium by each balancing the excesses of the others, and the system in consequence takes on a rigidity that makes it intolerant of views outside of itself. As a result, what began as an effort to find a viable middle ground between idiosyncrasy and prescriptiveness succumbs to its own rigidity.

A contemporary critic, Wayne Booth, made even more overt efforts to limit the scope of the reader's interpretive latitude. Booth, in the extremely popular *Rhetoric of Fiction*, goes beyond limiting one's options for assessment and explicitly relegates the reader to a position inferior to that of the author and his or her work: "Regardless of my real beliefs and practices, I must subordinate my mind and heart to the book if I am to enjoy it to the full. The author creates, in short, an image of himself and another image of his reader; he makes his reader, as he makes his second self, and the most successful reading is one in which the created selves, author and reader, can find complete agreement."[15] To conform to Booth's characterization, a reader has to accept not simply authorial intentionality but authorial hegemony in the discernment of meaning. While this provides neat, manageable guidelines for reading, it gives Booth's mode of interpretation an unhealthy authoritarianism that stands as antithetical to the individuality of the reader's experience.

In stark contrast, Kenneth Burke pushed the interpretive process informed by Cartesian thinking as far as conceivably possible toward the multiplicities and indeterminacies generated by the act of reading. Burke's methodology uses an approach similar to the dynamic tensions that Frye employed, but it emphasizes the way that language shapes human motives. In his determination to contextualize linearity, his willingness to blur distinctions between literature and nonliterature, and his insistence that a critic best understands literature by comprehending its effect upon readers, Burke anticipates the concepts that would wield so much influence in post-Structuralist thinking. Indeed, like Deconstruction theory, Burke's dialectic methods fully acknowledge the volatility of words and in consequence never completely overcome anarchic tendencies inherent in the language that he engages. For Burke "unification is not unity but a *compensation for disunity*" (Burke's emphasis).[16]

He goes on to lay out the mechanics of the dialectic process in a fashion that clearly recognizes its limitations:

> In strict accordance with dialectical principles, we may expect that the laws we discover will "transcend" previous laws, in proportion as the new conditions differ from previous conditions. And *furthermore*, as a corrective on empiricism, we shall be reminded that *our instruments are but structures of terms, and hence must be expected to manifest the nature of terms.* That is, we must always be admonished to remember, not that an experiment flatly and simply reveals *reality*, but rather that it *reveals only such reality as is capable of being revealed by this particular kind of terminology* (Burke's emphasis).[17]

There is much in Burke that vivifies the experience of reading, for his writing shows a wide-ranging interest in any number of topics, a great flexibility in modifying existing ideas, and a striking lack of concern for the absence of closure in any system he posits. Indeed, I think it no exaggeration to say that Burke's approach took an understanding of interpretation as far as it could go given the inherent limitations imposed by the Cartesian system of logic that he followed.

Burke was the last innovative thinker to challenge the status quo without recourse to the tenets of post-Structuralism, a range of movements loosely affiliated yet strikingly distinct. While Jacques Derrida's Deconstruction stands out as the post-Structural methodology still most often associated with the changes alluded to above, most of the work of Roland Barthes preceded Derrida's and reflects a much freer range of thought. Two books in particular, S/Z and *The Pleasure of the Text,* best reflect the demands and the rewards of the system that he advocated. In *S/Z* Barthes differentiates between the innovative *scriptible* (writerly) fiction and the classical *lisible* (readerly) fiction. Barthes emphasizes the tendency of *lisible* fiction to put the reader in the passive position of merely receiving information: "To end, to fill, to join, to unify—one might say that this is the basic requirement of the *readerly*, as though it were prey to some obsessive fear: that of omitting a connection."[18] As evident from this passage, early on Barthes had a sure sense of the dynamics of reading. In *S/Z*, however, his approach still reflects a sense of a power residing within the work to determine the nature of an interpretive response: readerly or writerly. Balzac's short story "Sarrasine" provides the frame that regularizes Barthes' views. In *The Pleasure of the Text* Barthes eschews that frame and cuts himself free from the restraints of cause-and-effect logic in articulating his sense of what he reads. In its place, Barthes simply offers what seem to be random impressions as a way of demonstrating the power of the individual reader to reconcile these apparent antinomies.

Whether it was because of the complexity of Barthes' approach, his untimely death, or simply the enthusiasm generated by Jacques Derrida, Barthes' views never gained widespread acceptance. In the end, perhaps the very nonlinearity toward which Barthes was moving put critics off. Indeed, those seeking radical alternatives to conventional theory but still wishing to have the anchor of a familiar logical system found precisely what they desired in the aggressive celebration of loss: Deconstruction.

Deconstruction, employing Newton's Second Law of Thermodynamics with a vengeance, pursues a relentlessly entropic approach to the nature of meaning. It focuses on tracing a trajectory of linguistic exhaustion in an effort to explain what happens in the process of reading. Deconstruction challenges the stability of any perception, teasing out internal contradictions as a way of invalidating whatever point of view it investigates. Its implicit claim, which allows it to dismantle so many alternative perspectives, is that any position not uniformly coherent stands as meaningless.[19]

Thus, the ideas of Deconstruction work effectively only within the system that it claims to oppose. The comprehensive strategies of Derrida's approach quite accurately discern points of linear contradiction within a piece of literature. However, his theories do not take into account that the significance of contradiction obtains only in a work operating according to a Cartesian, cause-and-effect system. A further irony emerges from any discussion of Deconstruction. Given that system's insistence upon the indeterminacy of language, according to its own premises, assessing it cannot extend beyond a subjective view. In essence, the act of propounding the theory of Deconstruction becomes a deconstruction of that theory. Deconstruction has never reconciled the clash between its impulse to read subjectively while speaking objectively. My study rests on the assertion that speaking subjectively is just as valid as perceiving subjectively. New interpretive standards can enable subjective views to make useful contributions to public discourse.

Deconstruction's methods question the integrity of language, and consequently its practitioners take issue with the presumption that language can convey any stable meaning. If the reader accepts this fundamental either/or proposition, then Deconstruction's nihilistic logic becomes depressingly formidable. In its closed system, it is possible to rebut Deconstruction's claims of indeterminacy only by using the vehicle, language, that it already presumes to be undependable. At the same time, with a nostalgia for order equal to that found in any of Samuel Beckett's characters, advocates of Deconstruction continually give primacy to the concepts of closure and of definitive meaning by their relentless examinations of the absence of these factors in reading.[20] Within its binary mode of thinking, in order to give indeterminacy significance, Deconstruction privileges its unattainable opposite.[21]

Just as Northrop Frye emerged in the mid-1950s as a voice seeking a middle ground between solipsism and prescriptiveness, by the mid-1970s two German critics were gaining popularity as figures offering mediation between the negation of Deconstruction and the utility of traditional criticism. Though by no means the only proponents of approaches generally grouped under the term *Reader Response,* Wolfgang Iser and Hans Robert Jauss provide a vocabulary that gives a unity and consistency to those methods both privileging the views of the individual and regularizing them in a systematic fashion.[22] Iser has offered a lexicon for discussing the various elements of reader response—figure, ground, succession, horizon, and latency—operating within the ostensive purport of an accepted repertoire of narrative segments. Too often, however, these terms fail to encompass the multiplicity inherent in a complex narrative. Iser speaks of the repertoire of a work: the familiar literary territory of social and cultural norms and the literary tradition from which it emerges. He sees the repertoire conditioning both the process of composition and our response, but he remains rather general in his assessment of how it occurs.[23] Jauss comes closer to an openness in perception in his concept of "horizon of expectations," but his sense of paradigm remains too static, too bound to linearity, to acknowledge the freedom inherent in an individual's experience with literature.

Stanley Fish has emerged as the advocate of reader response best known to Americans, yet Fish's conceptions of reader response have a much greater hierarchical bias and prescriptiveness—as in his identification of the interpretive community and invocation of the ideal reader—than those of either Iser or Jauss.[24] While Fish keeps vague his description of these terms, he cannot relinquish the hope of achieving a definitive interpretation. In the end, his approach seeks simply to privilege his way of seeing a work rather than to reflect the range of views of readers in general.[25]

Finally, as both an extension of Deconstruction and a reaction to it, cultural critiques arose, seeking to extend the significance of a text through associations with complex social systems. These approaches owe a great deal to historians like Carlo Ginzburg, who, in *The Cheese and the Worms*, shows how a thoughtful analyst can write against stereotypical responses to a familiar historical event (in this case the Inquisition) yet retain the ability to reach conclusions and initiate investigations based upon concepts of the event that the writer and reader share.[26] Literary critics like Stephen Greenblatt have followed similar modes of examination by remaining attentive to various elements of the social repertoire, as in the features of sixteenth-century England that he sees manifested in Shakespeare's plays.[27] Nonetheless, a persistent aura of ideological determinism inhibits these views. Greenblatt can be very clever in pointing out the manner by which historical context enhances the range of meanings of a work, but he cannot avoid the inherent exclusionary consequences of the specific cultural agendas that he implements by choosing what to highlight or what not to highlight.

Despite the critiques that I have made, I readily admit that each of the approaches outlined above functions as a highly sophisticated and, within its parameters, an extremely effective means for interpreting literature. At the same time, each methodology relentlessly deletes what are perceived as extraneous elements to produce an explanation of a work's function that conforms to the critic's specific point of view. Like the blind men describing the elephant, each topical or ideological effort at criticism tends to distort perceptions of the work under consideration, and each produces a fragmented impression that never blends into a complete picture. Sometimes these views are linked, producing a false sense of multiplicity by overlooking the contradictions in the competing critical approaches, but in fact these amalgamations take on a hierarchical form and in the end give primacy to a single perspective.[28] To have relevance for more than a select few whose subjective responses come close to the critic's own, formal readings need to adopt patterns of reading followed by any individual. This means applying a nonlinear, nonexclusionary, open-ended approach.

In this study, I am seeking neither closure nor indeterminacy. Rather, I am endeavoring to articulate a strategy that enables a genuine acceptance of pluralism, one that reflects the way reading encounters literature. This means advancing a system of criticism grounded upon the way a typical reading simultaneously sustains a range of different responses to a work without giving primacy to any.

2   Nonlinear Thinking

Redefining the Paradigm

The artist, like the God of the creation, remains within or behind or beyond or above his handiwork, invisible, refined out of existence, indifferent, paring his fingernails.
JAMES JOYCE

[God] does not play dice with the universe.
ALBERT EINSTEIN

THE TWENTIETH CENTURY witnessed a radical reconfiguration of the way that individuals understand the world around them. The most striking changes first appeared in material apprehension. From Einstein's work on relativity to research on chaos and complexity, scientists began to recognize elements in our physical environment imperceptible to approaches based upon Newtonian modes of inquiry. These discoveries in turn have led to reconsiderations of the fundamental assumptions informing science's perception of the world. Humanists, sensing the broad applicability of these concepts, also have striven to incorporate aspects of this new way of thinking into their work. The New Physics, which has already had an impact upon the way we think in general, also has specific application to literary criticism, as the procedures of nonlinearity can be employed for a better accommodation of our needs as readers.

Joyce and Einstein, because of their monumental achievements in their respective fields of art and science, offer prime examples of what can be accomplished by individuals capable of adopting logical systems that develop beyond traditional Newtonian or Cartesian thinking. As we come to an understanding of how these men, and others using similar methods, formulate and then articulate their views of the world, we approach a clearer sense of how to overcome the limitations imposed by traditional habits of thought and expression. The epigraphs of this chapter illustrate what I mean by the way that Joyce and Einstein thought. In contrast to those committed to conventional analysis, each cultivated a facility for sustaining multiple perspectives. Both quotations reference a universe functioning simultaneously on physical and metaphysical levels. Both trace connections between fixed and fluid conceptions of materialism and spirituality. And finally, in juxtaposing the ambiguous proposition of an ultimate cause and the apparently certain sense of a palpable framework, both passages suggest imaginative options for comprehension open to those who disregard the linear exclusivity of standard inquiry.

Obviously, any attempt to reason according to protocols followed by Joyce or Einstein faces certain difficulties. Many within the humanities still feel a strong affinity for the linear approach of deductive reasoning. As noted in the previous chapter, common habits of discerning the world in terms of cause-and-effect associations make it difficult even for those advocating the most innovative interpretive methods to adopt analytic modes that avoid exclusionary thinking and instead privilege multiplicity.

At the same time, new ways of configuring the physical world offer models that can overturn the hegemony of cause-and-effect thinking. From the discoveries of Einstein to the present work in theoretical physics, scientists have reconfigured conceptions of our surroundings by finding connections in antinomies that commonplace, Cartesian thinkers see only as contradictions. Through an accommodation of ambiguity foreign to more conventional approaches, writers like Steven Weinberg, in *Dreams of a Final Theory*, and James Lovelock, in *The Ages of Gaia*, for example, move toward recognizing an order in the universe that scientists following Newtonian methods cannot hope to discern.[1]

Of course, change in any discipline progresses slowly, and these alternatives remain difficult for materialist scientists working within the Cartesian tradition to accept. Thinkers like Weinberg and Lovelock rely upon an attitude that seems closer to theological faith than to Enlightenment empiricism in their efforts to bridge analytical gaps in systems of understanding. While striving to maintain a secular perspective, both scientists grope for basic, all-encompassing explanations of the complexity of creation, in different ways positing an organizing principle that they believe to be present yet cannot delineate.

Nonetheless, this shift from traditional ways of viewing the world, while predictably unsettling, in fact follows the cyclical form of development that has always characterized innovative thinking. Every approach to innovative interpretation must rest upon evolving, provisional assumptions or succumb to paralysis, and no exclusionary system of perception can hold a privileged position indefinitely. In the early Middle Ages, for example, Scholastics, responding to the explosion of knowledge created by the reappearance of Aristotle's writings and the introduction of Greek and Arab works of science and philosophy, attempted to create a system of thought based upon multiple sources of truth. To order their world, they placed the truth of revelation above that of reason and the truth of reason above that of praxis and of art. Embracing Mystery in Catholic dogma, they had no need for the linear certitude that eschewed a pluralistic worldview. In fact, Scholasticism thrived upon multiplicity.

Perception exists dynamically, however, and over time Scholasticism inevitably came under the duress of shifting points of view. The Enlightenment dismissed the Scholastics' approach to knowing the world as imprecise and superstitious. Cartesians, rebelling against what they saw as a privileging of uncertainty, strove to find definitive conclusions. The rise of cause-and-effect thinking powerfully enforced a new mode of reflection, applied uniformly by thinkers in any number of disciplines. This approach banished mystery and symbolism and eliminated all sources of truth other than the line of reason. Newton codified this effort with his laws of physics, and subsequent thinkers embraced those precepts as the source of a rich metaphoric system of images.[2]

These transitions, of course, never form discrete entities. Just as Scholastic thinking continued to exert influence well into the Enlightenment, Cartesian metaphors display a sustained hold on our discourse, particularly in descriptions of the environment surrounding us. The tenacity of this condition seems singularly perplexing, considering that around the beginning of the twentieth century the basis for this imagery lost considerable scientific legitimacy as the paradigms for perceiving the universe shifted again. Mathematician Jules-Henri Poincaré and physicist Albert Einstein, though operating quite independent of one another, called into question the infallibility of Newton's assumptions about the material world and laid the foundation for the development of the distinct though related concepts held in quantum physics and chaos theories.[3] New hypotheses led away from either/or thinking, and an interest in plurality reasserted itself.

From this revised point of view, exclusionary inquiries lost their primacy, and instead nonlinear views gained credibility. Simple inputs often led to complex results, and, consequently, the possibility of making accurate predictions of results based upon a perceived sense of their causes became increasingly unlikely.[4] (While this is not the place to recapitulate the history of the last one hundred years of science, I realize that for some readers these references may seem arcane. For a survey of the scientific achievements of the early twentieth century, see the appendix.)

Over the past few decades, humanists looking for alternative interpretive paradigms have endeavored to bring to bear on their disciplines the analytical implications of post-Einsteinian scientific thinking. A number have sought to transfer the concepts of chaos and complexity theories and other aspects of the New Physics into their disciplines.[5] The work of N. Katherine Hayles, especially *Chaos Bound*, has deservedly gained the greatest attention from humanists interested in exploiting this new interpretive paradigm. Hayles uses post-Einsteinian scientific thought to derive methods for interpreting contemporary literature that address assumptions of a post-Modern aesthetic.[6] Once she has outlined fundamental concepts of chaos and complexity theories, she applies them to explanations of interconnections in science, literature, and other features of the culture. Hayles makes clear distinctions between her humanist methodology and that of the hard sciences, and consequently avoids the trap of attempting to work out exact correspondences between disparate humanist and scientific concepts of chaos. Instead, she offers broad paradigmatic parallels as a way of suggesting a vocabulary for literature akin to that which delineates physical phenomena.

Another literary critic, Harriett Hawkins, in a work that frankly builds upon Hayles's efforts, expands the application of chaos and complexity.[7] Hawkins moves deftly between the seventeenth and the twentieth centuries, drawing parallels between the works of Shakespeare, Milton, and selected contemporary writers. Like Hayles, Hawkins realizes that the mathematical equations underlying chaos and complexity theories will prove daunting to most readers, and so she offers a useful introduction to the fundamental concepts of science and a good transition to the application of these views to literature, without going to extremes like trying to impose mathematical correspondences that probably do not exist. What truly distinguishes Hawkins' work, however, is her ability to go beyond the relatively narrow limits of contemporary writing and discipline-bound thinking to move easily back and forth between the sciences and the humanities. With a refreshing openness she points out the rich metaphoric potential within the discoveries of post-Einsteinian science and offers judicious examples of the useful application of nonlinear dynamic thinking in this broad fashion.[8]

Philip Kuberski, working contemporaneously with Hayles and Hawkins, offers provocative propositions regarding the application of scientific principles to the study of literature.[9] Kuberski's book focuses closely on reconceptualizing post-Modernism through definitions that emphasize its stochastic yet deterministic features. In a rigorous yet engaging fashion, Kuberski outlines new conjunctions of science and literature, informed by Deconstruction and post-Einsteinian thought. Although Kuberski relies too heavily upon a generalized impression of Deconstruction that ignores its mechanistic tendencies, his analogy suggests a propitious beginning for developing the metaphoric associations that he has identified. William W. Demastes, in *Theatre of Chaos*, provides a more balanced approach, focusing on readings of post-Modern theater from the perspective of chaos theory.

Overall, the work of critics like Hayles, Hawkins, Kuberski, and Demastes has already had a profound impact on approaches to post-Modern literature. As already mentioned, however, our habits of reading make it necessary to extend their studies. Problems of multiple interpretive potential and of inadvertent selectivity arise even in writings that on the surface appear distinctly more conventional.

Because a piece of literature resembles a complex and chaotic system — an entity with overall order yet made up of components acting in a seemingly unpredictable fashion — ostensibly minor variations in perception have significant long-term impact. Ignoring certain details, no matter how seemingly trivial, circumscribes our options for understanding a work. At the same time, like the meteorological consequences of the animation of the butterfly noted in the appendix, engaging these details, in whatever way we choose to, has an exponential impact upon our response to all that follows.

The act of reading underscores simultaneously the instability and the purposefulness of any piece of literature. Understanding its potential means sustaining rather than eliminating options for comprehension.

Post-Structuralist critics have been saying as much for three decades. However, because of their affiliation with linear thinking, they have not offered successful models for implementing this approach. Employing nonlinear concepts from the New Physics can alleviate this problem. I am not attempting to impose Einstein's General Theory of Relativity or Heisenberg's Uncertainty Principle on an interpretation of *David Copperfield* or some such work. I am instead demonstrating how the application of nonlinear analytic forms opens literary criticism in much the same way that it opened physics.

Acknowledging the coexistence of competing, complicated forces within a realm of perception stands as a good first step toward understanding our options for talking about literature. Think of a drop of water moving apparently indiscriminately within the predictable flow of a river. In the entities under consideration, despite the perception of erratic behavior, more often than not organization exists in some form and at some level. At the same time, discovering it more often than not requires a shift in conventional habits of comprehension. Recognizing the arbitrary aspects of the act of reading does not suffice to reform habits of criticism, for that recognition in itself only underscores the linear development of meaning. With each arbitrary choice, the options open for subsequent choices narrow, and the system becomes increasingly exclusionary.

Viewing a literary work as a chaotic system disrupts the prescriptive, narrowing impulse of the conventional interpretive approach that continually tightens its focus as it moves toward a specific conclusion. Such a single-minded comprehension ignores as extraneous any elements that do not fall within the realm of its argument and compels the unsatisfactory choice between either inconsistent or reductive readings.

An example from *The Picture of Dorian Gray* illustrates this point. Deciding that the first chapter of the novel describes the title character as a victim, rather than a hero or a villain, changes our perception of him in all subsequent episodes. We find it difficult to reconcile the image of Dorian as a victim (because he has been seduced by Lord Henry's description of New Hedonism) with his destruction of Sybil Vane, his blackmail of Alan Campbell, and his angry assault on the painting that has dominated his life. Categorizing Dorian as a villain or hero proves no less restrictive, for contradictions to these roles also abound throughout the novel. Instead, we need a method that will encompass all variables. Acknowledging that he simultaneously inhabits all three personae frustrates efforts at imposing closure even as it attenuates the pleasure that Wilde's novel affords. When we let go of the need to resolve antinomies within the narrative and instead enjoy the way that they contrast with one another, the range of pleasure afforded by the work increases exponentially.

Even with the complex fluctuations in a work of literature, however, some cohesiveness still obtains, and post-Einsteinian physics provides models for comprehending the organization at the heart of apparent disharmony. Perhaps the most useful concept critics can borrow is the willingness of scientists simply to accept the overall harmony of a system. I do not need, for example, to find a logical predictability in the movement of every molecule in a river in order to understand that river as a clearly defined entity with fixed borders and a predictable flow. As readers we need to cultivate a similar breadth of perception. By accepting as implicit the unity of a piece of literature existing within the boundaries of the artifact in front of me, I can proceed to discuss its diverse features without the burden of accounting how each relates to the other. Once I decide that it is not my responsibility to respond to literature in a Cartesian fashion, my formal interpretations will come to resemble the immediate uninhibited experience that I feel in reading.

At the same time, accepting a measure of randomness within a unified narrative does not mean reading without a purpose. When scientists study the most chaotic of systems—turbulence, for example—by using models outside of conventional forms, they can still find patterns within apparently arbitrary movement. While they cannot predict the path of specific molecules in an agitated liquid, they can see a discernible order. In these instances phenomena called strange attractors define the flux. These strange attractors stabilize chaotic systems, keeping them from expanding into infinity. If I trace the paths of various objects in the chaotic system, I find that, while they never occupy the same position twice, they remain within fixed boundaries and maintain orbits in a nonperiodic, or irregular, fashion. This is because, as Stephen H. Kellert notes, strange attractors reconcile the apparently contradictory effects of these objects.[10] Although strange attractors are not discernible through conventional scientific procedures, chaos/complexity theory proclaims their existence through the pattern that emerges from infinite paths moving within a confined space.

That image suggests an effective strategy for my efforts to interpret a novel as seemingly complex as *Ulysses* or one as apparently straightforward as *The Good Soldier* in a coherent fashion, without succumbing either to anarchic responses or limiting readings. Despite the potential complexity of any novel's narrative, finite anchors—often sensed by the reader rather than actually delineated—exist for the wide range of meanings that I might generate from various readings. The image of the strange attractor illustrates the overall process of reading that sustains multiple nonreplicating meanings—

all circumscribed by the boundaries laid down by the finite words selected
by the author—and the play of approximate but never duplicate images that
it excites in the readers' minds. Further, chaos/complexity theory has shown
me that I need not labor over a strict delineation of this attractor, but instead
I can go on to examine its effects on my readings.

Thus, no matter how many different, even contradictory, factors shape
the personality of Stephen Dedalus—imbued by his Catholic upbringing,
traumatized by his family's descent into poverty, invigorated by an inquiring,
artistic mind—I can discern a single consciousness to which to relate them.
The essence of Stephen's nature remains ambiguous, for I can never fix its
weight or assign to it the specific function of these and other features. Nonetheless, by accepting the cohesiveness that his consciousness gives to
Stephen, I can explore the contradictory aspects of his nature without jeop-
ardizing my sense of the unity of his existence. I have a clear reference point
for my views on Stephen that consistently reminds me of the personal nature
of those opinions. Likewise, recognizing the unity of the distinctive natures
of Leopold and Molly Bloom provides me with more than adequate anchors
for comprehending their conflicted consciousnesses.

As is the case with many phenomena observed in the physical world,
words are both unstable and also sensitive to slight variations in initial conditions. Thus, if I perceive the opening line of *The Good Soldier*—"This is
the saddest story I have ever heard"[11]—as tinged by an ironic tone, this earliest opinion will have an effect upon my sense of everything that John
Dowell, the narrator, says thereafter. Dowell's pronouncements about his
wife, Florence, about the Ashburnhams, or about anyone else in the novel
will convey to me multiple and often contradictory impressions. By the close
of the novel, this view has transformed my initial image of Dowell as long-
suffering cuckold into a picture of him as a sadistic, manipulative pervert.
Likewise, assuming the antithetical position of taking the opening at face
value produces a very different coloration. Dowell emerges as a man, admit-
tedly of limited intelligence but fundamentally decent, wounded by despair.
From this perspective, the more I hear of his story, the more inclined I am to
perceive him as a clearly tragic figure. Dowell becomes for me a sympathetic
character imposed upon by a calculating and uncaring wife and manipu-
lated by ruthless acquaintances who see him as a pawn in their struggles with
one another.

Selecting either position would mean applying common interpretive
practices. That, however, too neatly ignores the central issue raised by the
ambiguity surrounding Dowell's opening statement. Like the movement of
light that simultaneously displays characteristics of wave and particle patterns of quantum physics, and, as a result, does not yield to analysis through
classical methods of science, a reader cannot fully explain a complex literary

figure like John Dowell by using conventional, either/or critical methods. These approaches, no matter how sophisticated, always omit something.[12]

Of course, the way that I have been regularizing these terms might give the impression that drawing upon ideas from chaos studies replicates identification of familiar thematic patterns that merely lurk beneath the surface. In fact, elements from chaos theory continually remind us that it describes conditions operating according to very different protocols of behavior. The way that a reader discerns the nature of a literary character and the changes that accrue in the reader's opinion of that character can result in a sudden reconfiguration of perceptions of that figure. What stands as most significant is not the shift from one judgment to another but rather what it does for the reader's awareness of the spectrum of alternatives through which that judgment passes. It is that spectrum and not the final conclusion that represents the richest aesthetic aspect of the work.

The concept of fractal basin boundaries illustrates this point quite clearly. In an area lacking distinguishing borders, this theory describes the margins differentiating between the points drawn to one strange attractor and the points drawn to another as an ambiguous transitional phase, not as distinct demarcations. Like an accumulation of water that will eventually cause a drop that hangs pendulously from a faucet to fall, conflicted impressions of a character accrue in a way that calls for a radical change in perspective even as it maintains temporary stasis.

Because apprehension evolves over the course of reading, shifts in awareness rarely occur in a smooth fashion. Rather, the residue of previous impressions intermingles with elements of emerging concepts. The image of the fractal basin, then, proves liberating as an alternative to the either/or thinking of conventional criticism that posits definitive differences between characterizations. The simplicity of selecting a designation for Hamlet—madman, revenger, malcontent, or any of a half dozen other labels—seems both less accurate and less satisfying when instead he is located in the literary equivalent of a fractal basin. Though Hamlet seeks to impose limits on his mania—"I am but mad north-northwest. When the wind is southerly, I know a hawk from a handsaw" (II.ii.405)—the distinctions within his nature in fact are much more complex. As Hamlet himself operates on the borders, with fluctuating motivations seeming to direct his behavior, my need to resolve the antinomies that arise diminishes and a greater freedom to luxuriate in them supplants that feeling. Indeed, he becomes more interesting to me if I amalgamate a view that has him as coincidentally mad, conniving, innocent, and confused. While at any point in the play I may give preference to a particular label, selecting one personality for Hamlet over the others emerges as a distracting conundrum. Accommodating the elasticity of various roles becomes far more important.

For some readers this fascination with ambiguity may suggest a contingent aspect in my approach that would seem to limit its usefulness to anyone but myself. However, the multiple perspectives that shape the level of individual interpretive decisions characterize all reading, and so elaboration of the experiences of one individual inevitably illuminates those of others. An analogue in the hard sciences, a phenomenon called scaling, helps the reader address the issue of how subjective responses can feature in literary criticism.

Scaling denotes formal repetition on various levels, manifested through images called fractals. Despite moving up and down in scales of size, the same fundamental structure defines the shape of a complex work. What happens at one level in scaling can affect another. Further, scaling replicates forms in vastly different contexts.[13] That means that scaling highlights formal affinities in areas where no thematic parallels exist. This phenomenon in turn points up a range of complementary responses when common protocols inform the constructions of topically different literary works.

Vladimir Propp, in his well-known study of fairy tales, attempted to articulate a similar concept, but the limitations of Formalism that shaped his analyses prevented this approach from developing beyond rigid categorization.[14] The underlying point of his work, however, touches upon an important fact. Reading, despite being centered upon the acts of an individual, comes out of a social context, and as a result no matter how personal one's response, the process still operates according to some common protocols.

Scaling provides guidelines for accommodating this condition. Unlike the reductive application of microcosmic and macrocosmic associations, scaling does not endorse the mechanistic anatomizing of literature, the search for a single rigid framework supporting diverse themes. Rather, it draws attention to the fundamentally congruent aspects of creativity throughout writing that nonetheless manifest themselves in sharply divergent artistic images. By pursuing the implications of scaling, readers can discover a complexity in works heretofore deemed banal and in doing so find aesthetic gratification where it previously had been hidden.

Thus, a Batman comic book, while initially bearing little more than a passing resemblance to more sophisticated writing, yields complexities through analogies to works more highly regarded. Similar narrative patterns appear in Batman's actions and those of the title character in *The Song of Roland*, for example—a hero set apart from all others, a villainous force or forces that only the hero can confront, a philosophy that sees destiny as a shaping force in one's life and in consequence urges behavior that reflects an acceptance of fate. Finding these analogues does not lead to finding meaning in *The Song of Roland* and the Batman comic in the same fashion, but it does stimulate efforts to see a complexity in the latter not heretofore evident. Indeed, scaling helps overcome a reluctance to accord merit to a commercially successful endeavor. It invites a reader to legitimize the response to less-esteemed writing as more than witty precociousness or deft contrarianism. Larger interpretive patterns validate the enterprise.

As always, of course, any effort to regularize form, no matter how unique, raises the possibility of producing prescriptive readings. The fundamental concepts in New Physics, however, forestall such predictability. Indeed, as demonstrated in Mandelbrot sets—figures that replicate basic patterns with great complexity at every level of examination—scaling does not simply call attention to similarities. It illuminates how the iteration of similar forms can produce profound differences. Though the pattern remains roughly the same, from level to level the replication increases and so produces forms of infinite variety. That is to say, commonality likely leads to elaboration, not simply replication.

Imagine, for instance, how I might take a term like *hero*, use it broadly to delineate a class of character across literature, modify that delineation to sustain generic integrity, continue to reconfigure that view from work to work, and see that sense changing yet again through multiple readings of the same work. Does my most recent conception of Tom Jones (the eighteenth-century English literary character, not the twentieth-century Welsh night-club singer) have any connection to the abstract concept of hero with which I began my ruminations? Yes and no, and this complements my delineation of reading as an act evolving in an unspecified way yet developing within discernible boundaries.

While Tom Jones is commonly labeled a version of the English picaro and in consequence neatly sorted among the range of possible heroic personae, that term has little direct value for the individual reader seeking to understand the process of finding meaning in Fielding's novel. Rather, it is more useful to realize that I built up my sense of Tom's character from the patterns that I have discerned in a long line of admirable figures—each character distinct yet each sharing the same designation. Reading about these individuals stabilized my generic sense of the term *hero*, even as it gave me an idiosyncratic comprehension of the word. The more heroes that I encounter in literature, the more forms contribute to the construction of the concept and the more flexible that conception becomes. At the same time, the more diversity I find, the more I strive to maintain continuity with the generic term. When placed in the flexible context of chaos/complexity theory, these seemingly mutually exclusive impulses in fact enhance my options for seeing and enjoying manifestations of the heroic figure in literature.

What I am advocating here is not a reconfiguration in our habits of reading but rather a new awareness of what we already do. Sophisticated readers

have learned to balance ambiguity with such dexterity that the process
moves forward without conscious effort. So far, formal criticism has not generated a metaphoric system that can articulate the complexities of that process. My efforts do not aim to dismiss the achievements of previous critics
but rather to introduce a vocabulary and an analytic method that allows
expansion of existing formal responses to literature.

Applying methods of nonlinear analysis to specific works of literature lies
at the heart of this new approach. To underscore that point, I have in the
following chapters linked a conventional critical form with each work, and I
have then contrasted the results of reading according to these protocols with
interpretations that come out of the methods that I advocate. Thus, I begin
in chapter 3 by showing that when I endeavor to illuminate *Finnegans Wake*
by placing it in its cultural context, it becomes circumscribed by very specific information, a limitation that, paradoxically, a more subjective reading
resists. A more satisfying response welcomes the associations that arise from
the social repertoire of Joyce's narrative, but it does not allow those associations to displace alternative ways of reading. This interpretation does not
simply accept the existence of alternative readings but affirms the need for
the simultaneous comprehension of them.

Of course, by beginning my argument with examples from *Finnegans
Wake*, I am taking a relatively easy course. For years readers have identified
Finnegans Wake as a text whose inherent complexity yields any number of
meanings. Nonetheless, as the paradigmatic post-Modern text—indeed, as a
work whose experimental structure has not been equaled by any subsequent
effort—*Finnegans Wake* stands as a useful first step in the demonstration of
the effectiveness of the approach that I advocate. In its form and content
Finnegans Wake embraces the same nonlinear thinking that I advocate in
my critical approach, and it has already proven a fertile source for theorists
seeking to demonstrate the efficacy of nonlinearity in literature.[15]

It is for that reason that I would do a disservice to my study to dwell exten-
sively on *Finnegans Wake* or other post-Modern works. The indeterminacy
of post-Modernism makes any work in that category a ready illustration of
the discursive multiplicity that I advocate. To show the true effectiveness of
a nonlinear approach to literature, I must demonstrate its widespread efficacy, especially in genres that seem on the surface to be the least suited to its
interpretive techniques.

Toward this end, in the remaining chapters I have self-consciously drawn
from works representative of traditional, rather than innovative, literary
forms as examples of the validity of my argument. As with my overview of
critical methodologies in the preceding chapter, this group does not stand as
an exhaustive survey. Rather, I have chosen works characteristic of diverse
popular genres, and I hope that my examination will provoke readers to

associations with still others. The point is not to cover all of the possibilities for application of nonlinear readings but rather to suggest the freedom with which I may employ this method to understand any work of literature.

In chapter 4 I take up *Harry Potter and the Sorcerer's Stone,* a work that both fits the conventions of fairy tales and has a narrative longer than most other works in the genre. Hence, it offers many more examples of how I can relate my approach to that form. In interpretations of *Harry Potter and the Sorcerer's Stone,* the archetypal and psychoanalytic methods traditionally applied to fairy tales create a prescriptive interpretation at odds with instinctive readings. In my examination, I aim to show how *Harry Potter and the Sorcerer's Stone* conforms to the conventions of popular fairy tale writing, and then, by suggesting the complexity that I can draw from readings, I demonstrate how this approach can foreground the work's imaginative possibilities.

Reading conditions us to derive meaning associatively, and we apply that technique as much to comprehend genres as to understand individual works. With this technique in mind, I take up in chapter 5 a form with clear affinities to the fairy tale, the epic. Although any number of works would serve as an example of epic composition, I have selected *Beowulf* because of its resonances with the literary tradition from which I emerge. Additionally, Seamus Heaney's extraordinary rendering of that work into modern English allows us to see the efficacy of nonlinear reading of fine poetry.

In my examination, I intend to show how the writing of an anonymous poet (or, as some critics have argued, poets) descending from an oral tradition yields much greater satisfaction when read from a perspective that accommodates its inherent diversity. As is highlighted by the Heaney version, it is the evocative and often contradictory images provoked by the language of *Beowulf* that give the poem its strongest imaginative appeal. Heaney's rendition beautifully illustrates how the denial of resolution, the invocation of nonexclusionary perceptions, opens the experience of reading *Beowulf* to sensations that conventional linear responses would never acknowledge.

While I believe that this approach will open both fairy tales and epics to interpretations heretofore ignored, a cursory survey of the criticism of these genres would show that even linear thinking has generated a variety of interesting responses to both genres. This diversity is not characteristic of every literary form, and I consequently wish to demonstrate the effectiveness of my approach when confronted with a text already circumscribed by canonical readings. In this case I have turned to the biblical account in the Book of Job. As I illustrate in chapter 6, even such innovative linear approaches to it as feminist readings provide only limited alternatives to the conventional responses to Job. In contrast, nonlinear thinking can reconfigure the work in a fashion that allows readers both to sustain reverence for it as a religious document and to enjoy the complexity that makes Job such a powerful story. (Indeed, though I will argue that engagement with Job does not require me to approach it as a theological document, it seems to me that the very ambiguity and inconsistency at the heart of my reading highlight the crucial aspect of faith central to religious belief.)

Finally, I will close my study by applying nonlinear thinking to dramatic criticism, with an examination of an issue—the nature of self—that stands at the heart of literary inquiry since the *Oedipus* cycle. On the surface, Oscar Wilde's stunning play *The Importance of Being Earnest* seems the embodiment of conventional dramatic writing. Even if a reader wishes to push the meaning of its witty lines from farce to satire, few critics until recently have chosen to make *The Importance of Being Earnest* anything more than the celebration of childishness and the sophisticated enumeration of the various ploys used by young men determined to resist the imperative to grow up. Lately, critics, especially those interested in postcolonial thinking, have begun to reassess the play's status. In chapter 7 I readily admit that *The Importance of Being Earnest* raises interesting questions regarding Irish identity, but I seek to push the dialogue further than seeing it as a polemic against imperialism. Indeed, as I hope to show, more comes from the characterizations if I show a willingness to eschew the impulse to fix on them the features of national traits and instead see their chameleon-like tendencies. It is in the very gesture of ostensive conformity that these figures represent Wilde at his most subversive, a trait difficult to discern from a linear point of view.

Overall, my goal in this study is to offer contrasting contemporary interpretations with readings based upon nonlinearity, upon a desire to sustain multiplicity, and upon a comprehension of unities that does not demand some form of exclusion. In this fashion I seek to demonstrate the way non-Newtonian thinking can draw the practice of criticism much closer to individual readings than has previously been the case. I endeavor not so much to impose meanings on the works under consideration here as to explore options for their interpretation. As artifacts in the conflicted position of having set boundaries (page length, sentence orderings, word choices that do not change from reading to reading) and open-ended perceptions (images that vary from reader to reader, passages that receive greater or lesser emphasis, concepts that are taken seriously or dismissed or ignored), literary works offer unique challenges to readers. My aim is to show that, while as readers we have consistently met those challenges, as critics we have suppressed our own best impulses, and we have presented reductive and simplistic renderings of these works.

3   **Reading on the Edge of Chaos**

Finnegans Wake and the Burden of Linearity

We are suspended in language.
NIELS BOHR

Finnegans Wake stands as the academic's version of the Bible: It is the book that most literary critics own, that some revere, and that few actually read. That disparity between possession and apprehension does not simply grow out of intellectual lethargy, however, for formidable hermeneutic barriers discourage efforts to engage Joyce's final work. Because the book's organization and content systematically frustrate explication through established critical procedures, a widespread inability to derive pleasure from reading *Finnegans Wake* matches the near universal sense of its grand significance.

Of course, not all readers feel daunted by the work. William York Tindall, Anthony Burgess, John Gordon, Danis Rose, and John O'Hanlon—to name just a few—have offered their strategies for comprehending *Finnegans Wake*.[1] However, to judge by the reactions of some critics, these studies have served only to highlight the various and fragmented responses people have had to Joyce's work.[2] More often than not, the reviewers who have criticized these guides object to what they see as oversimplifications of the book. While that argument certainly has some validity, it is hard to imagine— given the dominant features of traditional criticism—any other results when critics rely upon conventional methods to articulate their sense of Joyce's final work.

The cause-and-effect logic that underpins traditional interpretive thinking simply cannot do justice to the complexities of *Finnegans Wake*. Joyce wrote his book with no regard for the boundaries imposed by Cartesian analysis. Consequently, any successful response to it must rely upon an alternative approach to reasoning, equally free of those limits.

This makes Joyce's compositional disposition of *Finnegans Wake* an excellent subject for the interpretive concepts derived from the New Physics. Because of the nonlinearity of *Finnegans Wake*, an analytic perspective that sustains multiple possibilities and avoids the prescriptiveness of exclusionary logic provides a more than amenable basis for engaging Joyce's prose. More specifically, a system that employs strategies for dealing with phenomena that enjoy infinite possibilities within precisely set borders directly addresses features characterizing the discourse of *Finnegans Wake*.

Perhaps the most striking consequence of post-Einsteinian scientific discoveries has been the tacit acknowledgment that the linear cause and effect of Cartesian predictability, which habitually conditions assumptions not just about physics but about the way that we process all perception, has lost its efficacy. Efforts to address questions like Benoit Mandelbrot's "How long is the coast of Britain?" for instance, went well beyond revisions of Newtonian mechanics and inevitably led to larger concerns about seeing the physical world.[3] Only in the last few years, however, have scientists begun to exploit the implications of this work by employing a vocabulary that recognizes and describes the pluralistic, multilayered aspects of perception. As late as 1958, Werner Heisenberg could confidently assert that "[t]he influence of the Cartesian division on human thought in the following centuries [after the publication of his *Discourse on Method*] can hardly be overestimated."[4]

A note of explanation is in order here. Throughout this study I use the terms *linear* and *nonlinear thinking* in a broad fashion that some scientists might find unsettling, and therefore it becomes important to clarify the application that I intend. In my sense of the phrase, linear thinking works according to exclusionary, cause-and-effect logic: one for one. It sees the whole as equal to the sum of its parts. It moves toward closure by seeking a single resolution to a particular problem. Nonlinear thinking eschews this sort of closure and seeks to sustain multiplicity: one for many. The whole exceeds the sum of its parts. It maintains a range of perspectives, and endeavors to promote multiple responses by refusing to privilege any one point of view over the others.

A number of useful concepts have grown out of this perspective. Field theory, for example, invites us to rethink the dependability of our perceptions by challenging the presumption that measurements are nonintrusive. It asserts that we cannot observe something without influencing that which we observe and hence influencing the outcome of every measurement that we make. Incorporating this concept into even the most conventional approach to literary criticism quickly strips away any pretense of objectivity or stability and instead draws attention to the mercurial subjectivity of the act.

An equally striking premise, the "edge of chaos" concept, disputes the validity of belief in movement solely by steady, regular increments from order to chaos. An icicle melting as it hangs from a gutter illustrates this concept. It does not dissolve at a regular rate but drips erratically and then suddenly crashes to the ground. This movement exemplifies the more chaotic evolutions, occurring through repeated and abrupt disordered changes from one system to another—a series of volcanic eruptions that produce an island in the middle of the ocean. By questioning assumptions of periodic entropy—regularity in the rate of decline—this view raises doubts about conventional approaches to understanding changes in the world around us (the Ice Age, the depletion of the ozone layer, the extinction of a species).

These ideas have far-reaching application to critiques of epistemologies employed by the humanities, for they supply vivid metaphors to support thinking in a nonlinear way. For centuries literary critics—like their counterparts in the sciences—have conformed to the expectations of a culture that has privileged linear, cause-and-effect logic as the most productive form of analysis. In consequence, the metaphors used to express critical concepts came out of this Cartesian orientation.

This approach has not gone unchallenged, and in the 1960s and 1970s Deconstruction seemed to promise an alternative approach. Unfortunately, although its practitioners proved adept at undermining existing systems of linearity, they could not provide a methodology that would not succumb to their own critiques. The periodic erosion that worked so well on others proved to be a nemesis to Deconstruction. However, Derrida and others did not comprehend that their critiques failed because they did not go far enough.

The consequence of circumscribed, linear thinking—analyses based upon systems that ignore concepts like field theory and "edge of chaos" changes—is that an exegesis often does not present an account of a full aesthetic experience with a work. Instead, what emerges is an abridged and adapted version emphasizing the validity of one or two impressions, a truncated reading at best. These conventional criticisms follow an exclusionary impulse that domesticates responses, highlighting only a few ideas and constructing linear arguments from only those portions of the material under consideration that are relevant to the support of that argument. This gesture parallels the reductivist thinking of classical science.

More useful readings, on the other hand, encompass the multiple responses that grow out of a creative engagement with words on the printed page. These impressions function like a series of directed explosions—imaginative bursts generated by the same source but with repercussions independent of that source and of one another. The nonlinear thinking that enhances comprehension of the physical world can also facilitate a far more sophisticated understanding of the multiplicity and pluralism of this aesthetic.[5]

Even before its final version appeared in print, *Finnegans Wake* inspired a striking interpretive exception to this tendency of a linear, exclusionary pursuit of meaning with the publication of *Our Exagmination round His Factification for Incamination of Work in Progress*. This 1929 collection of essays by Samuel Beckett, Eugene Jolas, Elliot Paul, William Carlos Williams, and other avant-garde writers demonstrates that the term *Work in Progress* (the prepublication title that Joyce used) can be applied with equal accuracy to the interpretive responses to *Finnegans Wake*.[6] Indeed, the diffused and distracted responses in this volume stand out not as flawed criticism but rather as subtle reflections of the multiplicity conditioning any sophisticated reading of that work.

Unfortunately, this early effort proved an exception to the predominant approach, and a pattern of linear thought has persistently reasserted itself in readings of Joyce's final book. Edmund Wilson's comments, for instance, written the year that *Finnegans Wake* was published, follow a reductive analogy into binary either/or categorization: "James Joyce's *Ulysses* was an attempt to present directly the thoughts and feelings of a group of Dubliners through the whole course of a summer day. *Finnegans Wake* is a comple-mentary attempt to render the dream fantasies and the half-unconscious sensations experienced by a single person in the course of a night's sleep."[7]

Harry Levin, in remarks made two years later, freely acknowledges the book's multiplicity, yet he simultaneously limits it through a conventional frame of reference. Even as Levin's citation of Aesop's blind men and the elephant lauds Joyce as capable of fully discerning that arrangement, it rel-egates other readers to at best a piecemeal comprehension: "Our attempts to criticize *Finnegans Wake*, in the two years since its definitive appearance, have been about as accurate and as adequate as the efforts of Aesop's blind men to describe an elephant. Lacking the full perspective that Joyce alone had eyes to see, we have been left with one of the white elephants of litera-ture. . . . Since no one [besides Joyce] can be trusted to unravel his fullest implications or construe his ultra-violet allusions or improvise his lost chords, every one else is relieved of responsibility."[8]

More than a decade later, William York Tindall turns to circularity as a strategy for overturning linearity. Unfortunately, he cannot get beyond lin-ear thought because he cannot set aside a circumscribed vocabulary. Efforts to use self-reflexivity to evoke the spirit of the work only become bogged down in tautology: "*Finnegans Wake* is about *Finnegans Wake*. That is this: not only about everything, the book is about putting everything down in records and interpreting them. . . . To say, then, that *Finnegans Wake* is about itself is to say that, including our reality, *Finnegans Wake* is about our ideas about it and they are *Finnegans Wake*."[9]

Clive Hart's highly influential *Structure and Motif in* Finnegans Wake is a book frankly devoted to tracing the fundamental design of the *Wake*. With a tone that conveyed unwavering confidence in its teleological view of inter-preting Joyce's final work, it set the pattern for three decades of exegesis: "I have had frequent occasion to discuss source-material throughout this book but my principal aim has always been to show how Joyce infused signifi-cance into his diverse raw materials by his use of closely controlled formal structures."[10]

In contrast, perhaps no critic of *Finnegans Wake*, writing prior to the ad-vent of post-Structuralist criticism, had a greater sense of the inadequacy of conventional approaches to it than did Bernard Benstock. His ground-breaking 1965 study not only underscores the shortcomings that others have noted (with a subtle play upon Wilson's metaphor), it also highlights a num-ber of other weaknesses in contemporary methods of reading. At the same time, Benstock seems resigned to the hegemony of familiar linear patterns of analysis: "No critic, however, can be certain that his efforts are any less blind than those of preceding Aesopians, or that his whitewashing will not leave just another dark coat. He must nonetheless make his original efforts in an area where trial-and-error criticism is the prescribed if precarious method."[11]

Vincent Cheng's thematic approach acknowledges an all-encompassing comprehension of *Finnegans Wake* as an unrealistic goal. Nonetheless, he too retains nostalgia for conventional methods of apprehension, albeit on a diminished scale: "The aim of this study is to establish beyond doubt the centrality and omnipresence of Shakespeare, of the Shakespearean corpus, and of the dramatic metaphor in *Finnegans Wake*, and to provide a useful reference work for *Wake* readers: a guide to Shakespearean usage and allusion in *Finnegans Wake*."[12]

David Hayman, whose commentary on the *Wake* spans five decades, very properly turns attention back to Joyce's process of composition. Nonetheless, the language of his discourse—"seeming randomness," "rational conclusions"—suggests an ongoing attachment to the methods of linear criticism:

> The present book is meant to contribute to an ongoing dialogue, but perhaps its special focus on a range of early traces will set it apart from other more general or more narrowly conceived projects. We will be examining those aspects of the creative process revealed by a study of the early notebooks and manuscripts in order to disclose how Joyce managed the transition from the diurnal to the nocturnal, the waking to the sleeping, the individual consciousness to the universal subconscious. In the process we will address the question of the seeming randomness of Joyce's note taking, establish relationships, study contexts, and attempt to draw rational conclusions concerning Joyce's methods at different moments in the book's early development.[13]

Even Margot Norris' pioneering early work, *The De-Centered Universe of Finnegans Wake: A Structuralist Analysis*, explored the possibilities open to nonconventional readings. In her more recent *Joyce's Web: The Social Unraveling of Modernism*, Norris seems drawn by ideological concerns toward an essentialist view of *Finnegans Wake*: "'Anna Livid Plurabelle' is a work song, with the women's labor of washing figuratively and socially inscribed in the lyrical, vulgar, idiomatic, robust speech produced within the social conditions and social relations of their work."[14]

I do not intend this catalogue, however, as a disparagement of individual readers nor as a dismissal of specific criticisms of *Finnegans Wake*.[15] Indeed, the scholars to which I refer in this chapter stand among the most eminent critics working on Joyce's writing. I do not take issue with any of their findings. I simply observe that their methodologies inhibit rather than enhance their ability to offer effective interpretations of *Finnegans Wake*.

Toward this end, I seek to highlight an issue more fundamental than the accuracy of a particular exposition. The problem facing readers of the *Wake*—though articulated in various forms—has always been the same: How can I acknowledge its complexity yet at the same time approach it with a system of criticism simple enough to encompass its magnitude? Because

Cartesian reasoning privileges logical consistency through clearly defined linear relationships, it serves as the default interpretive response to *Finnegans Wake*. In fact, this approach inhibits analysis. It suppresses impressions that do not fit the patterns created by this methodology, and by leaving out ostensibly unrelated observations from the criticism, it produces an artificial rendering of natural reader response. We comprehend the complexity of *Finnegans Wake* through complicated models of discernment, and efforts to articulate those models according to a linear form prove hopelessly simplistic.

Thomas Jackson Rice, in an approach similar to those literary analyses pioneered by both Hayles and Hawkins, has written thoughtfully about the way that complexity theories help readers understand the structure of *Finnegans Wake,* and the difference in our aims underscores the thrust of my project.[16] Rice scrupulously adheres to a system that translates the methods of New Physics from science to the humanities without any modification. He endeavors to show that a humanist can apply the concepts of the New Physics with a rigor equal to that of any scientist. Nonetheless, I think the discoveries of post-Einsteinian science offer even more to humanists when they apply the concepts in a fashion suited to the protocols of their discipline rather than according to strictures imposed by the hard sciences.

New Physics stands as a rich source of interpretive metaphors that liberate readers from programmatic thinking. It provides a wealth of images that allow us to think nonlinearly. I do not wish to show that I can examine literature by using ideas from the New Physics in the same way that a scientist would study turbulence in a stream. I do not seek to avoid rigor, but I do wish to preclude prescriptiveness. I want to apply New Physics on my own terms to explore how complexity theories describe a paradigm that fits a typical response to *Finnegans Wake:* a way of organizing meaning that extends across a range of interpretive positions. My aim is to emphasize the idea that patterns of reading for almost everyone adhere to an epistemology shaped by nonlinear complexity. From this view I take the position that formal criticisms that do not reflect that condition simply fail to address aesthetic experience.

To illustrate my assertion that I see much more in a work by adopting a nonlinear point of view, I will contrast it with the approaches taken by various critics to identifying figures in the "St. Patrick and the Druid" episode (*FW* 611.04–612.36).[17] This passage describes Joyce's version of an encounter well known in Irish folklore between St. Patrick, Leary, the High King of Ireland at the time of St. Patrick's missionary efforts, and the Archdruid who represents pagan Ireland. In the ensuing struggle for supremacy between Christian and pagan beliefs, St. Patrick prevailed and was given permission to preach in Ireland. Joyce's version retains the fundamental details of this exchange while overlaying them with thematic and formal concerns that characterize the narrative of *Finnegans Wake*.

The passage was one of the first that Joyce composed, and as early as the summer of 1923, in letters to Harriet Shaw Weaver, he singled out St. Patrick as a pivotal figure in the episode.[18] Since then, discussions of St. Patrick and of his conversion of the Celts to Christianity have come to dominate criticisms of the passage.[19] This glossing provides the immediate satisfaction of affording readers a body of clear-cut information arguably related to a most difficult portion of Joyce's book, yet the framework of passages like this and certainly the aesthetic informing all of *Finnegans Wake* resist the restricted readings that a single perspective produces.

An essay by Riana O'Dwyer gives a wonderful example of how a critic can imaginatively exploit associations with St. Patrick, but her study also highlights the consequences of readings that explicitly or implicitly use linearity to move toward closure.[20] O'Dwyer examines Stefan Czarnowski's *Le culte des héros et ses conditions sociales: Saint Patrice, héros national de l'Irlande*, a book that Joyce was enthusiastically recommending during his early work on *Finnegans Wake*.[21] Over the course of her study, O'Dwyer lays out a sophisticated, scholarly assessment of Joyce's paradigmatic use of Czarnowski's concepts of the hero: "especially for the development of characterization within the cosmic historical and philosophical framework on which [Joyce] wished to build his new world epic, and for its interpretation of Irish society which justified Joyce's own use of Ireland as the stage for the creative expression of man's eternal rise and fall."[22] In the process O'Dwyer shows the range of figures from Celtic mythology evoked by the passage's narrative references to St. Patrick.

O'Dwyer's work plausibly represents the way that the associative structure of *Finnegans Wake* enables specific figures to produce archetypal resonances throughout a passage. At the same time, employing such a system imposes the inevitable consequence of narrowing a reader's responses to the figure of St. Patrick. As with any linear method, the role or category assigned to St. Patrick as an archetype then precludes any reading that falls outside these very sharply defined parameters.

A less-encumbered response to the passage's representation of St. Patrick—and one more accommodating to the multiple impressions created in a reading—comes when the reader takes into account the religious dogma associated with the allusion. For those familiar with Christian folklore, the St. Patrick reference evokes the apocryphal story of the saint's use of the shamrock to explain to the pagan Irish the doctrine of the Blessed Trinity, a reference that Joyce's narrative simultaneously highlights and calls into question when his Patrick displays a "synthetic shammyrag" to enact that theological lesson (*FW*, 612.26–31). That in itself may seem a dead end until the implications of this association come under consideration.

As Joyce well knew, the power of the Catholic Church's teachings on the Trinity centers on its identification as a Mystery—something that Catholics cannot fully understand but must accept as part of the beliefs of their religion. Father Robert Boyle stands out as the best commentator on the use that Joyce made of Catholic teachings in his writings, and Boyle has highlighted the impact of references like this throughout *Finnegans Wake*.[23] Nonetheless, I think it worth revisiting this Trinitarian allusion via St. Patrick to note how very neatly it evokes the complex function of referentiality in the discourse of the *Wake*.[24]

If in reading this passage I move self-consciously from the life of St. Patrick to the doctrine of the Trinity—from loosely verifiable fact to complete mystery—then I have acknowledged an important feature of the way that fact illuminates the reading that I might derive. The Trinitarian image of three persons in one God remains a concept that a Catholic sustains without ever fully comprehending. As writers like St. Augustine have demonstrated, however, rather than frustrating contemplation of the essence of Divinity, this dogma has provided both the goad and the latitude for wide-ranging thought.

Analogous conditions exist in complexity studies, and secular critics averse to embracing this apparent mysticism should keep in mind the dogged determination of scientists to come up with a Theory of Everything.[25] That is to say, a Theory of Everything acknowledges an observable world that the researcher does not fully understand, yet it posits the existence of a fundamental organizing principle. From this basic supposition, scientists project complex operational mechanisms, illustrating the procedure already cited, that intricate results often grow out of elementary principles. It also demonstrates that a partial or imperfect discernment of basic principles does not preclude intellectual engagement.

Paradoxically, acknowledging an incomplete understanding of ultimate causes enhances opportunities for understanding. Observations function at the broadest imaginable level of aesthetic perception. The viewer does not automatically exclude any response because it does not fit an already determined pattern of criticism, nor is any response privileged because it complements a particular linear reading. Both the Mystery of the Holy Trinity and the Theory of Everything resist interpretive resolution in precisely the way that extratextual references do in *Finnegans Wake*. Allusions in the *Wake* do not dispel ambiguity; they create it. The imaginative associations that they provoke increase the diversity of readings rather than limit them through categorization. Glosses can to some degree act as contextualizing influences, but they can never fully explain the discourse between reader and author produced by the narrative.

Nonetheless, the nostalgia for closure exerts a powerful force on those forming an understanding of the passage. Like many of the Irish who might have heard St. Patrick's analogy between the Trinity and the shamrock, some readers affirm a belief in multiplicity and then seize upon a simplistic representation of it, endeavoring to dispel complexity in favor of a reductive view. Nowhere is this more apparent than in criticisms of *Finnegans Wake* that seek to dispel rather than sustain the diverse allusiveness of the work. An examination of the allusions to historical events evoked by the narrative discourse throughout Kate's tour of the Willingdone Museyroom (*FW*, 8.09–10.23) shows how this occurs and how it can be avoided.

The museum—an amalgamation of real and imagined historical repositories in England, France, Belgium, and Ireland—features a collection of memorabilia from the battle of Waterloo. Kate's tour of the building, however, evokes much more than a reconstruction of the events of that battle and a representation of the personal conflict between Wellington and Napoleon. By touching upon struggles from the Peloponnesian War to World War I, its survey of Western civilization as evidenced through conflict stands as both densely historical and wildly anachronistic.

Over the years, a number of scholars have provided extremely thorough glosses of cultural references that recur throughout the Museyroom passage.[26] The justification for such efforts rests upon the presumption that they enhance one's ability to enjoy that portion of the narrative, and countless readers have endorsed that premise in turning to these glosses. This approach loses much of its effectiveness, however, when reductivist certitude characterizes the application of the citations. In fact, echoing the limitations already noted regarding Newtonian science, assumptions about the applicability of historical allusions in the Museyroom passage of *Finnegans Wake*— or, for that matter, in any work of fiction—can actually inhibit imaginative responses to the narrative. Indeed, contemporary conceptions of plurality challenge such objectivist scholarship, implicitly raising questions regarding how a linear awareness of the events at Waterloo and a knowledge of the other battles to which the narrative refers enhance aesthetic enjoyment or understanding of the Museyroom tour and, by extension, of the work as a whole.

Popular views relate interpretations of any historical event to an overall pattern of analysis that conforms roughly to the precepts of Newtonian mechanics: an observer can discern the elements that constitute a particular event and then apply cause-and-effect logic to understand how those elements interacted to bring about the specific incident. Conventional historiography moves from kinesis to stasis, from chaos to knowledge, adhering to

Clemenceau's portentous warning—echoed by Santayana—that those who do not learn from history are condemned to repeat it.

Of course, recently some historians—without necessarily using the vocabulary of chaos/complexity theory but nonetheless following the spirit of its central premise—have vigorously reexamined the basic suppositions that form the foundation of such methodology. Taking inspiration from the hard sciences, they have established useful paradigms for nonlinear interpretation. Michel de Certeau, for example, has energetically called into question the belief in objectivist history.[27] Unfortunately, de Certeau's optimistic assertion of the demise of this way of thinking has proven to be premature. Although scholars have seen the flaws in objectivism, many still read history—or at least the events narrated by like-minded colleagues—as the pursuit of certitude and the invocation of closure. The drawbacks of this attitude become accentuated when scholars apply principles of historicism to literary exegesis. In fact, the very success of critics like Stephen Greenblatt in their advocacy of New Historicism—which is merely the old historicism read on a microcosmic level—rests upon a willingness to apply reductionist manifestations of history to literature.

Let us instead consider an expansionist view of possibilities. This does not call into question the incorporation of historical material into a reader's response. Quite the contrary, it takes issue with the restrictive way that some critics apply history to literature. Stephen Dedalus' rebuttal of Clemenceau's positivistic views by calling history "a nightmare from which I am trying to awake" (U, 2.377) stands only as the first step.

In Ulysses Stephen rejected the concept of historical linearity, but at the same time could not adapt to the ambiguity of its alternative. This condition remained for him anarchic and threatening. The nonlinear representations in Finnegans Wake, on the other hand, delineate a paradigm that both rejects linearity and embraces complexity. The Museyroom episode and the responses that literary critics have made to it nicely illustrate this process.

One of the earliest and still most exhaustive studies of this passage came from a forty-five-page exegesis compiled by Philip Lamar Graham, Philip B. Sullivan, and G. F. Richter and published in the July and October 1962 issues of The Analyst, "'Mind Your Hats Goan In!': Notes on the Museyroom Episode of Finnegans Wake."[28] It moves through the narrative of the Museyroom passage with painstaking care, giving readers information derived from a line-by-line, phrase-by-phrase, even word-by-word examination. The Graham, Sullivan, and Richter essay makes no interpretive connection between their glosses and Joyce's narrative, and thus it maintains the spirit of complexity that I advocate as the most useful interpretive response to a work. Graham and his coauthors presume that all of the information contained in the passage—that which is historically accurate and that which is anachronistic or misleading—has a similar effect: It all contributes to the images that provoke the reader's imaginative response. A commitment to complexity regulates readings not according to immutable concepts of historicity but rather according to a sense of its antinomies. We perceive in a nonlinear rather than a linear fashion. Therefore, forcing allusions imbedded within the discourse into a symmetrical pattern moves me no closer to a coherent articulation of an aesthetic response to the passage than where I was before undertaking all of this research.

Using these glosses as a linearly organized overlay for criticism remains a popular approach. Summing up the Museyroom episode, Danis Rose and John O'Hanlon call the passage "a complex description of the objects in the building (which we realise may be the Wellington monument itself or no more than a horse mushroom sprung up overnight), a tour conducted by Kate the keeper-guide. Inside the museum scenes from the age-old battle(s) are commemorated in wax. These waxworks, carefully juxtaposed, tell a tale of sexual jealousy; the saga of 'Lipoleum jiminy/Willingdone'."[29] I may freely acknowledge the logic and insight of this synopsis, and at the same time observe that it nonetheless limits consideration of other complex elements within the passage. That is to say, Rose and O'Hanlon interpret not incorrectly but insufficiently. They and others who adhere to this procedure have not yet found a way to offer an encompassing view of this or any other portion of *Finnegans Wake*. Surely, it is not sufficient simply to say that all criticisms remain partial readings, for such a position merely offers a rationalization for circumscribed thinking.

Our alternative, of course, is not to dismiss all of the annotative work that has already been done. Nor should we simply pretend that information about references occurring in *Finnegans Wake* could have no aesthetic significance. Instead, we can respond to information derived from the narrative in a manner that refuses to sacrifice multiplicity for a kind of clarity, or ambiguity for a systematic tidiness.

A paradigm for such patterns of reading emerges from Edward Lorenz's meteorological models.[30] The aperiodic climatic conditions represented on Lorenz's graphs move through a series of dispositions that never repeat themselves yet remain within the boundaries of a precisely defined system. Because slight variations in temperature, air pressure, humidity, or other features can lead to a geometric impact upon the weather—the aforementioned Butterfly Effect—forecasting with accuracy is nearly impossible. Likewise, repeated readings (by the same person or by different individuals) of a selected literary passage will never lead to the same aesthetic experience, because variable aspects of the interpretive process—experience, imaginative disposition, emotional connotation, and other elements— change the response radically. The results of readings—like the weather itself—cannot be predicted with accuracy. Thus an observer needs to establish aperiodic protocols—nonlinear guidelines for comprehending non-repetitive conditions—and the image of the Museyroom itself provides a handy humanist model for such a project.

The function of a museum suggests useful ways for setting such parameters. A successful museum exhibit offers snapshots of a culture rather than summations. It extends self-consciously subjective experiences and frankly acknowledges its own idiosyncrasies and biases. Consequently, no reasonable viewer would abrogate the authority to rebut, refute, or revise conclusions implicit in the display.

This does not mean that museum exhibits are fraudulent or invalid. Nor does it mean that they are hopelessly solipsistic. Rather, such displays consistently enforce their nature as works in progress. They present implicit invitations to their viewers to elaborate upon the creative process begun by the exhibit's curator, but they are not framed in a way that dictates the form viewer responses will take. They trigger responses and give the viewer isolated bits of information, but, again like the weather, their makeup cannot be fully understood in a rough linear discourse.

Applying this attitude to an interpretation of the Museyroom episode means extrapolating responses from impressions within the episode without necessarily linking these impressions in the syllogistic form followed by conventional criticisms. Since this mode of reading eschews readings set in a self-contained narrative form, we can assign pivotal roles in our responses to the relentless punning, to the battle allusions, to the sexual tension, or to any other elements within the passage without having to suppress all of the other referential reverberations within the work. One element in the narration has no more inherent worth than any other. Allusions within the discourse function as would any other artistic expression. Diverse features disrupt not in a rigid Formalist fashion of programmatic defamiliarization but in the manner of Barthes's playfulness. Identifying these elements makes us aware of how we read rather than attempting to limit what we read.

From such a perspective, knowledge of historical figures alluded to in the Museyroom passage can have a catalytic but not prescriptive effect on interpretation. The word *lipoleum*, for example, suggests by its commonness the sort of multiplicity that allows the narrative of *Finnegans Wake* to function so effectively. The glosses in *The Analyst* essay identify it with such disparate biographical figures as Napoleon, William of Orange, and James II. Each connotation undermines the one preceding it without eliminating its continuing effect, exemplifying Derrida's twin gestures of deconstructing a term and of placing it under erasure. This serves not so much as a validation of post-Structuralism but rather as a reiteration of the nonhierarchical, impermanent character of the *Wake*. The polyphony of its narrative insistently overturns the hegemony of traditional historical discourse, just as, with every reading, it reorders the impact of particular images. Paradoxically, acknowledging the range of historical allusiveness within the term *lipoleum* helps break the tendency to stratify responses or to privilege a single interpretive view.

Of course, it is difficult to sustain simultaneous contrasting imaginative responses to Kate's tour. A reader may go so far as to follow a linear method of muting the resonances of specific words or images in order to remain more attentive to others. The reader may not, however, draw this idiosyncratic view into a public response and seek to legitimize it as an exhaustive interpretation through an appeal to historical authority. To do so would simply ignore too much of the text.

This "commodius vicus of recirculation" brings me back to the central element of my protocols of reading *Finnegans Wake*: the need to retain a sense of its mystery through models found in contemporary physics. Neither the shammyrag of St. Patrick nor the historical glosses of the battle of Waterloo explain the *Wake*'s mystery. The reference guides so painstakingly compiled by a range of deservedly respected Joyce scholars serve as important resources for those engaged in reading *Finnegans Wake*. At the same time, they no more summarize the work than the *Baltimore Catechism* encompasses the complexity of the Catholic faith. Although adherents of reference guides and of catechisms will quickly assert that these works were not meant as a substitute for deeper meditation, those familiar with either or both are well aware of the ease with which readers use them as a justification for cessation of further study.

As I have already noted, Heisenberg's Uncertainty Principle—and indeed all of quantum mechanics—reminds us that we cannot simultaneously measure position and velocity or mass and speed, and the field theory explains why: Objectivity disappears when the observer is part of the system, for one's very presence adds a variable to what is being examined. This observation has both material and metaphysical application to criticism. If we persist in ignoring this condition of indeterminacy that stands as an integral part of any reading, we will find ourselves continually frustrated in attempts at conventional comprehension. A more satisfying experience with the text can come only if we adapt our goals to reflect what we do have the power to know.

The text of *Finnegans Wake* fits the description of any dynamic nonlinear system: "locally unpredictable, globally stable."[31] Responses to it—whether made in public or in private—retain a viability and validity in direct proportion to their resistance to conventional epistemology. The revelations of nonlinear dynamics remind us of the inaccuracy of slipping back into Cartesian patterns of reasoning. At the same time, the organization of chaos/complexity theories gives to models of reading a measure of purpose that deconstructive nihilism cannot provide. In the end, we do not so much need new interpretive habits as simply the willingness to assess our impressions in a fashion that accommodates the way that they already occur to us. Allusions that we discover in *Finnegans Wake* can lead to criticism that will most represent our aesthetic pleasure when our writing acknowledges chaos as commensurate with clarity, and complexity as preferable to closure.

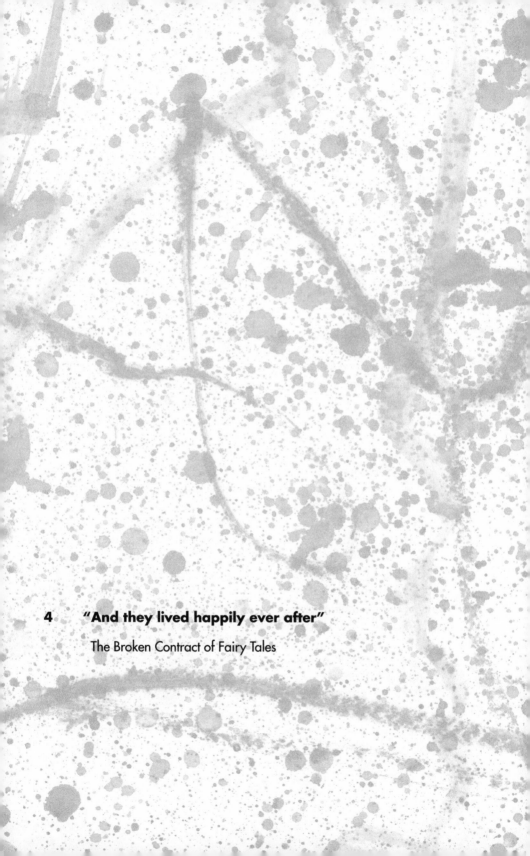

4 **"And they lived happily ever after"**

The Broken Contract of Fairy Tales

If one wishes to speak about the atomic particles themselves, one must either use the mathematical scheme as the only supplement to natural language or one must combine it with a language that makes use of a modified logic or of no well-defined logic at all.
WERNER HEISENBERG

FROM SOCIETY TO SOCIETY over the course of history, folklore has functioned in a consistent and readily recognizable role. It serves as a source for metaphors that give literature its distinctive flavor. It enacts important cultural concerns. And it translates the abstract values of the society into comprehensible images. Folktales consistently represent struggles of the weak against the strong, the exploitation of the disenfranchised by the privileged, and the dismissal of the marginalized by the accepted. In any society, folklore, along with its counterpart, mythology, represents the rudimentary values and fundamental conflicts of the culture. It stands as the oldest example of a literary tradition, and it acts as the foundation of all that supersedes it.

All this does not mean that the works that emerge from this genre follow a homogeneous pattern. Despite broad similarities in form and content, the protocols for the representation of folktales change from culture to culture, making each effort the product of a distinct and complex tradition. From the folklore of Aesop, to the fantastic accounts of Celtic mythology, to the bawdry of medieval fabliaux, to the legends of Paul Bunyan and Johnny Appleseed, each society has imposed a personalizing stamp on its folktales. Thus, though superficial similarities exist, for example, between the story of George Washington chopping down the cherry tree and that of the Spartan boy who stole a fox, the imaginative context from which each tale emerges requires a unique interpretive approach.[1]

Three hundred years ago, a surge of interest in the preservation of such stories made readers forcefully aware of the conflicting demands made by tales set in different cultural contexts, as the makeup of folklore shifted from an oral to a written folk tradition. In the late seventeenth and early eighteenth centuries, antiquarians, interested in conserving folklore by recording accounts in written records, began to collect and transcribe as many stories as possible. This effort made a range of different tales much more available than at any time previously, and also, through the collection and dissemination of different examples from the folk tradition, it challenged the comfortable interpretive habits that people had derived for finding meaning in the folklore of their community.

Additionally, the process of preserving oral accounts in print changed more than just our awareness of folktales. Anthologizing the stories that had been sustained for generations by word of mouth produced a significant degree of modification in the narration. Men like the Grimm brothers and

La Fontaine did more than simply transfer the tales from a vocal to a written medium. Indeed, in most cases their efforts at preservation radically altered the makeup of the stories they collected, reflecting as much the nature of the way the editors read as it did the features of the original act of composition.[2] In the process, the modern fairy tale came into existence.

From the beginning, anthologists worked to produce a regularizing effect. They sought to assimilate folktales into a recognized literary canon, and collectors standardized principles for classifying and ultimately for interpreting the stories, principles that continue to shape the approaches followed by most contemporary readers. Specifically, this regularization has led to an interpretive procedure that employs the same methods of explication given primacy by conventional literary criticism.

This preference for conventional procedures goes beyond an affinity for the familiar, for the adoption of those methods came as part of a broader effort to establish the validity of the study of fairy tales. Approaches to collecting and categorizing fairy tales have followed a consistent pattern over the past three centuries. At the same time, the current widespread acceptance of fairy tales as constituting a bona fide literary form came about only after a long period of intense scrutiny. Western society's attitude has only gradually evolved into the benevolent view of the genre that exists today.

Figures from the Enlightenment did not trouble to conceal their distaste for the fairy tale's implicit critique of utilitarianism. The Victorians considered the literary merits of fairy tales as negligible until the work of authors like E.T.A. Hoffmann and, of course, Hans Christian Andersen pushed the imaginative sophistication implicit in folk narrative into greater prominence. Perhaps the real turning point in attitudes in English-speaking countries, however, came about in the late nineteenth century, when writers such as Andrew Lang, John Ruskin, Charles Kingsley, and Oscar Wilde did much to establish the reputation of fairy tales within the literary ethos of the period. Once this legitimacy had been achieved, the practice of seeing fairy tales as worthy of study only for the linguistic information that they preserved from oral tradition gave way to formal, unified interpretive approaches of the works from conventional literary perspectives.[3]

An unfortunate consequence of this rise has been the formalization of the analytic process. Whatever meaning emerges for specific fables, the methods used for deriving interpretations have led to a characterization of the genre within a relatively rigid structure. More often than not receptions of modern fairy tales feature unambiguous articulations of the values informing the stories. They highlight sharply defined characters. They rely upon a liberal use of fantastic elements to move the plot forward. And they achieve a clear resolution of events at the conclusion of the narrative. Most readers accept the tightly defined, highly domesticated structure of the stories, and these elements, in turn, evoke a reassuring predictability in the way that the story unfolds. Indeed, Stephen Sondheim's musical *Into the Woods* derives much of its appeal precisely because of the way that it closely inverts the seeming inevitability of the moral world that emerges from traditional perceptions of fairy tales.

All this does not deny that certain specific changes have occurred in the way that we have come to read fairy tales. Over the course of the past century, the same kinetic interpretive features that have acted upon other areas of literary studies have had shaping effects upon efforts to assign meanings to fairy tales. However, those modifications have still occurred within the sharply delineated constraints of traditional methods.

This means that, despite some diversity, all of the methods functioned within the broad interpretive paradigms operative since the time of the Grimm brothers. Thus, with a highly prescriptive form as the basis for readers' experiences, responses to fairy tales generally still adhere to an approach as rigid as conceptions of the structure of the stories themselves. Criticisms typically follow a pattern of close readings. They presume that a dominant ethical concept unifies the narrative of each story, and they seek to discern it through careful examination of the central thematic issues of the work.[4] Even among those critics who allow for historical and ideological differences from reader to reader, this method, according to Maria Tatar, remains the prevalent influence shaping contemporary criticism. She asserts that "almost all of us turn to children's stories with the expectation that morals and lessons will be forthcoming, even in those cases where they are not spelled out in the text."[5]

Of course, within the broad conventions of traditional literary criticism, some noteworthy shifts in critical perspective have arisen over the years. The advent of Modernism at the beginning of the twentieth century, for example, reconfigured the hierarchical order within the ethical systems in which various readers situated the stories, even as the crucial features of their narratives remained fixed. Modernist sensibilities ensured that the traditional Judeo-Christian values, implicit in commentaries of the eighteenth and nineteenth centuries, no longer automatically conditioned all responses, although even Modernists assumed that a single discernible moral imperative, albeit one open to the subjective construction of the individual reader, informed a tale. All in all, whatever hermeneutic specifics obtained, a broad commitment to seeking a framework based upon exclusionary, linear thinking continued to dominate critical thinking

The most significant change in thinking during this period, however, was a shift to reading fairy tales for what they reveal about language: that is, a concern for stylistic rather than thematic interpretation. The work of Vladimir Propp imposed a syntagmatic, Formalist approach to folk and fairy tales.

First appearing in 1928, Propp's *Morphology of the Folktale* broke from traditional linguistic scholarship and laid the groundwork for reconsidering how to delineate the characteristics of the literal construction that defined the form of a tale. By mid-century the anthropologist Claude Lévi-Strauss countered Propp's examinations of the features of specific works with a paradigmatic, proto-Structuralist system that found generalized stylistic relations across the genre.[6]

In recent years, well after the paradigmatic shifts of Propp and Lévi-Strauss, a number of contemporary readers have advanced more directive techniques for exploring meaning within the genre, and in doing so they have shifted emphasis back from the linguistic construction of the tales to examinations of their imaginative content. Marxist or materialist critics, exemplified by Jack Zipes, have focused on the social constructs within and surrounding the tales. Much to the chagrin of many scholars in the field, psychoanalytic readers, perhaps best exemplified by Bruno Bettelheim, have appropriated the genre and used it to exemplify theories about how to assess the experiences and emotional life of children.[7] And even more recently, ideological critics have gone about refining approaches to the linguistic, materialistic, or psychoanalytic concepts of fairy tales to produce feminist responses, cultural critiques, and New Historical reassessments.[8]

Nonetheless, despite the focus of attention shifting between language and imagery, the overall interpretive approach to fairy tales has remained strikingly unchanged. For most critics, understanding fairy tales involves a comprehension of how each of us first came to give meaning to the world around us. While scholars like Jack Zipes and Bruno Bettelheim have disagreed as to the nature of that educative process, they are in accord that, for most of us, fairy tales represent the earliest form of story with which we became familiar.[9]

Personal experiences endorse these views. Our parents replicate their childhoods by telling us familiar fairy tales at bedtime from the time we are old enough to comprehend them (and sometimes even earlier). Teachers—from day-care centers through kindergartens and beyond—use stories from the fairy-tale heritage as the basis for exempla of how children should interact both in the classroom and out of it. And across a range of media, popular culture increasingly draws images from fairy tales as a shorthand means for evoking particular feelings, responses, or identifications.

Few would deny this pervasiveness. Further, because of their popular application within our culture, we all have come to recognize certain thematic and structural features in fairy tales that serve as definitive aspects of the genre. They are stories of fantastic events, experienced by figures whose characters are defined by one or more associated attributes (such as courage, honor, duplicity, or jealousy), and played out in a fashion that leads to a clear-cut and generally successful conclusion for those characters delineated as good.

The electronic media have done much to shape the contemporary view of fairy tales, and numerous critics have decried this phenomenon as a corrosive force undermining the integrity of a genre that they hold in the highest regard. In his early study of fairy tales, *Breaking the Magic Spell*, Jack Zipes, for example, notes the efforts of serious scholars to combat what they saw as the insidious influence of Disney and other mass marketers of the fairy-tale ethos: "As early as 1944 Horkheimer and Adorno demonstrated in *Dialectic of Enlightenment* the ways and means by which the culture industry employs technology and instrumentalizes reason to extend the domination of capitalism and make human beings and their cultural expressions into commodities."[10] It is possible to understand and perhaps even to sympathize with the frustration that Zipes and others feel over what they perceive as the dilution of works that they have identified as profoundly important. Nonetheless, a blanket dismissal of the renditions of these works by popular culture misses an important point in terms of the attitudes of the general reader.

Whether or not a reader or viewer disapproves of what Walt Disney Productions has done to Sleeping Beauty, Pinocchio, the Little Mermaid, or any other fairy-tale character, these versions have made a profound impact upon the general conception of fairy tales. Although they may have blunted the harshness of the elements in the original tales, their real influence emerges through a much more conventional gesture. Making the fairy tales much more accessible (what home with small children and a videotape player does not have a copy of at least one Disney version of a popular fairy tale?) has significantly reinforced conventional ways of seeing fairy tales. This influence in turn has underscored common forms of interpretation, and it is that which should command our interest.

At the same time, mass marketing fairy and folk stories has further inhibited efforts to understand the full complexity of the genre. The uniformity of Disney production values serves to mask the inherent ambiguities in the tales that I have already noted. Despite the variety of stories and the evolutionary impulses that periodically reshape the genre, most readers or viewers recast fairy tales in objective terms. They associate the works in this genre with a familiar, unproblematic narrative form. They see in this designation a rigidly defined structure for formulaic discourses elaborating a fixed number of themes.

For readers satisfied with applying the conventional critical approaches and committed to the assumption of an objective interpretive process, the same fundamental categories of goodness and evil, heroism and cowardice, nobility and baseness recur from work to work and serve as important guidelines for what and whom we should admire and what and whom we should despise as the narrative unfolds. These characteristics ensure that, though the details surrounding plots and individuals may change from work to work, for most readers the manner in which these stories unfold and the determination of what figures represent which values remain highly predictable.[11]

This predictability presents a formidable challenge to the interpretive methods that I am advocating. In this chapter I examine a work that operates within the conventions of the fairy tale, but that is formed completely from the modern consciousness and that has become a commercial success strictly by capturing the imagination of modern readers. *Harry Potter and the Sorcerer's Stone*—the first volume in the highly popular series of J. K. Rowling's children's books centered around the title character—conforms in general to the requirements of a traditional fairy tale, but it also emerges as the product of a thoroughly contemporary imagination.[12]

I do not wish the selection of *Harry Potter and the Sorcerer's Stone* as an example of how chaos theory can illuminate readings of fairy tales to seem a contrived effort at whimsicality or preciousness. Rather, I see the first installment in the Harry Potter series as a good example of a work clearly within the fairy-tale genre. The story evolves as popular fantasy. Its aim is to employ fantastical images and supernatural figures for entertainment. It stands as a repository of clearly articulated values. And it is narrated in a fashion easily accessible to a wide audience. Furthermore, it has the advantage that, whatever the expectations that I might bring to *Harry Potter and the Sorcerer's Stone*, I still read it without struggling with the accumulated interpretive history that necessarily surrounds older fairy tales.

Because it is a relatively new tale and is still unfamiliar to many readers, even after the success of the recent film version, I present a brief synopsis of the narrative before discussing possible responses. While the aim of this synopsis is simply to offer an overview, it implicitly highlights the features that mark *Harry Potter and the Sorcerer's Stone* as a fairy tale. This in turn underlines the link between contemporary fiction and the folklore tradition.

Like many fairy tales *Harry Potter and the Sorcerer's Stone* begins with the introduction of a protagonist whose antecedents are surrounded by ambiguity. A series of strange events marks as unique one day in an otherwise mundane routine of life in a nondescript English town—a cat reading a map, strangely dressed people milling about the town center, countless owls flying around in the middle of the day. Through these initial images the story establishes its authenticity through the deft juxtaposition of the quotidian and the bizarre.

That evening a wizard named Albus Dumbledore brings the infant Harry Potter to the doorstep of number four Privet Drive, home of Mr. and Mrs. Dursley, Harry's aunt and uncle. Dumbledore has singled out Harry for attention because, although only a baby, he has recently survived an attack by the renegade wizard Voldemort that took the lives of his parents. Dumbledore leaves Harry with the Dursleys for protection. Unfortunately, though hardly unexpectedly in a fairy tale, for the next ten years Harry lives in isolation and drudgery, imposed upon him by his aunt and uncle and punctuated by the bullying of their son, Dudley. All this begins to change on the eve of his tenth birthday, when Harry receives an invitation to attend wizard's school at a place called Hogwarts. Their disaffection for their nephew and their aversion to all things magical cause the Dursleys to expend a great deal of effort to prevent Harry from learning of this. However, when Harry does not respond to repeated invitations, the school sends Hagrid, Keeper of the Keys and Grounds at Hogwarts, to inform Harry of this offer, to enlighten him about his background and notoriety, and to prepare him to attend. Intimidated by Hagrid, the Dursleys find that they have no choice but to allow Harry to go to Hogwarts.

On the way to his new school, Harry meets Ron Weasley and Hermione Granger, and these introductions, by emphasizing all that Harry does not know about wizardry, allow for a measure of exposition that explains the history of Hogwarts and a number of the central aspects of wizardry to Harry and to the reader. At Hogwarts, the aura of fatalism, characteristic of many fairy tales, emerges early on as the magical Sorting Hat assigns the new students to one of four residential houses within the school. Each house serves as a center of academic and social life, and each reflects certain behavioral idiosyncrasies that characterize the nature of the students in the house. As the description of the daily routine at Hogwarts continues, the narrative elaborates upon the different types of classes that those at the school attend. It shows Harry making two enemies—Draco Malfoy, a student, and Professor Snape, a member of the Hogwarts faculty. The narrator at this point introduces the mystery of the third-floor corridor that Dumbledore, the school's headmaster, has put off-limits to all students. In the final segment of this intermediary stage, another characteristic fairy-tale feature emerges: the hero's discovery of a heretofore hidden or unknown power. In this case, Harry finds that he excels at Quidditch, a game with many of the characteristics of soccer and rugby but which is played high above the ground, with participants riding on flying brooms.

In short order, a series of events draws Harry, Ron, and Hermione into a commitment to unravel the enigma of the third-floor corridor. An invisibility cloak, once owned by his father, facilitates Harry's efforts. With the aid of the cloak, he discovers the eponymously named Mirror of Erised, a looking glass that reflects the viewer's desires on its surface. Additionally, the trio learns of the existence of the sorcerer's stone, an object with powerful rejuvenating capabilities, and they realize that it is hidden somewhere beyond the third-floor corridor. In trying to acquire more knowledge about the stone and its location, Harry, Ron, and Hermione must deal with distractions such as Hagrid's infatuation with a Norwegian Ridgeback Dragon, the ambivalent assistance of the Centaurs and Unicorns who inhabit the woods adjacent to the school, and the normal, if sometimes mysterious, routine of the school. All their efforts are further complicated by the presence of Voldemort, striving to gain control of the stone.

As the story draws to a close, the three friends commit themselves fully to thwarting Voldemort's efforts. They penetrate the secrets of the third-floor corridor, and Hermione and Ron each plays a pivotal role in the efforts to protect the stone. Harry, of course, takes on the bulk of the task. When he gets to the stone, Harry learns that Professor Quirrell, whom the trio had thought was working to protect the stone, is in fact Voldemort's pawn, and Professor Snape, whom they had suspected of treachery, has been trying to foil Voldemort's efforts. After a struggle with Quirrell and the spirit of Voldemort, Harry, with the assistance of Dumbledore, succeeds in saving the stone. The story ends with Harry's house winning the competition for the school's championship cup, and Harry preparing to return to the Dursleys' home for the summer, now armed with a great deal of self-confidence and a good working knowledge of magic.

Readers familiar with the conventions of such stories will have little difficulty seeing in Rowling's book an implicit invitation to make the formulaic fairy-tale response. In its opening pages, *Harry Potter and the Sorcerer's Stone* presents a familiar narrative paradigm that introduces a downtrodden central figure unaware of a magnificent destiny established by events in the past. Following the archetypal pattern, the book then traces the journey of the hero toward enlightenment and success. For readers who see this format as the only organizing structure worth attention in a fairy tale, understanding the subsequent narrative becomes merely a matter of identifying the traits that distinguish the central characters and then of explaining the behavior of these figures in terms of how they conform to particular types.

Certainly, *Harry Potter and the Sorcerer's Stone* highlights many familiar concepts found in traditional critical approaches, and, because of its length, it evokes a wide range of conventional expectations by conforming to the different prototypes laid down by a number of important fairy tales. For instance, Rowling's work follows the pattern of maturation found in such narratives as *Beauty and the Beast, Pinocchio, Cinderella,* and *Puss in Boots.* It also proves to be a parable of good versus evil, emphasizing lessons on how the upright person contends with the corrupt. In this way it stands as analogous to the discourse of *Snow White, Sleeping Beauty,* or *Little Red Riding Hood.* Additionally, it offers homey lessons on coping with the formidable social forces that attempt to shape the lives of its characters, similar to the narratives in *Jack and the Beanstalk, Aladdin and the King of Thieves,* and *Hansel and Gretel.*

With its extended narration, the discourse of *Harry Potter and the Sorcerer's Stone* lends itself to a number of familiar modes of reading fairy tales. Tracing concepts of good and evil, for example, allows separation of characters into one category or another. Individuals may be weak willed or strong, and in some instances, as in the narrative of *Hansel and Gretel,* commitment to one value system or another may seem to vacillate.[13] Nonetheless, a consistent, if sometimes undefined, sense of good and evil stands as the foundation of conventional readings applied to this and all other fairy tales.

Based upon this categorization a reader labels the actions of the characters with approval or disapproval. After some consideration of the matter, however, the difficulty in fixing guidelines for judging the traits of a particular character as good or evil emerges. Hard and fast rules, like the Ten Commandments, do not serve as the best standard for assessment. It becomes difficult, for example, to decide how to apply "thou shalt not kill" as a guide for judging a character's behavior when almost any individual in a fairy tale proves capable of performing the most violent of acts. Gretel pushes a woman into an oven. Jack takes the life of the giant by chopping down the beanstalk. Numerous characters considered heroes or heroines trick or swindle others. To differentiate between good and evil when considering seemingly identical acts of savagery requires a standard of subjectivity not easily reconciled with conventional Judeo-Christian ethics. In fact, even in the most prescriptive approaches, relativity dominates.

Context rather than behavior will designate a role. Figures who find themselves isolated, outside the power structure, and often, though not always, poor are generally labeled good. (Certainly, these features originally would have had an innate appeal to an audience of ordinary folk who might experience these same conditions.) In some instances, goodness is simply decreed by the narrative. In all cases, once a person is labeled good, his or her actions cannot overturn that designation. Quite the contrary, that label alone remains sufficient to absolve him or her from the judgment that might ordinarily accrue to behavior.

That concept has an important stabilizing role in conventional perceptions, for it allows readers to render neutral other attributes or actions that they would under normal circumstances see as highly negative and, consequently, as disruptive of a unified view of a character. For instance, violence, often combined with cunning, frequently acts as an important factor in regulating what seem to be unfair or disproportionate advantages in the fairy-tale world. When the narrative describes a society structured in a way that proves inadequate to deal with injustice or inequity, violence seems the only operative alternative for the protagonist. The intervention of a force with preternatural or supernatural power brings this condition to a crisis (*Sleeping Beauty*), and the protagonist of a fairy tale resolves this crisis either through some application of that preternatural or supernatural power (*Snow White*) or by a clever manipulation of the character who possesses it (*Rapunzel*).

I can easily apply to *Harry Potter and the Sorcerer's Stone* the sort of reading that conforms to the pattern outlined above. It will produce a straightforward, conventional view of events in the story. Characteristic of so many fairy tales that play upon ideas of damnation and redemption, *Harry Potter and the Sorcerer's Stone* begins with a seemingly sharp distinction between the preterit and the elect, those who inhabit the wizard world and those who live as muggles. The fact that Harry, a wizard, begins the tale trapped within the muggles' power structure immediately sets him apart as a heroic figure.

Within the wizard's world, distinctions between good and evil also relate to power but on a more complex level. The transgressions of Voldemort involve his efforts to overturn the benevolent hierarchy of the wizard world and to replace it with his own tyranny. In this respect he assumes the form of a Lucifer figure. At one time a most promising wizard, he has fallen from grace by defying the authority of goodness. Though defeated in direct confrontation, Voldemort now goes about the world seeking to seduce others to his cause. This casts the wizard world into something like a prelapsarian society or, at the very least, should the reader wish to sustain the biblical analogy, as a chosen people who preserve the true faith. Though their lives are by no means Edenic, the wizards nonetheless adhere to a strict set of codes that set them apart from the lower orders and that affirm their righteousness in the face of Voldemort's viciousness. The hermeneutic influence of Judeo-Christian mythology has long played a prominent part in shaping interpretations of Western folklore.

Voldemort is not the only figure used to define by contrast the world that Harry inhabits at Hogwarts. The narrative encourages readers to see the ordinary folk, derisively called "muggles" by both aspiring and successful wizards, as creatures insensitive to the rarer, more refined, and far more exciting world of the wizards. As in the tradition of biblical redemption of the elect who embrace the right way and the preterit who reject salvation, muggles by their ignorance live in contrast to the wizard world and forever stand outside the realm of perfectibility. They are like the beasts of the field—dumb and in most cases unwitting witnesses to the drama that unfolds within a higher order. The term *muggles* has an unpleasant aura surrounding it, and it requires no strain to see the analogy between racial or ethnic slurs and this designation. The point is not to indict the Rowling book but rather to underscore how relativity and contextualization can make permissible behavior that in another setting readers would never accept.

From this perspective the conclusion of *Harry Potter and the Sorcerer's Stone* stands as foregone. The conventions of the genre demand that, no matter how fierce the struggle or how close the side of goodness comes to defeat, in the end it must triumph. Indeed, Harry's victory remains of secondary significance. Of real importance, from the perspective of the archetypal fairy-tale narrative, is the refining process by which a young hero like Harry matures to the point of being worthy to defeat the evil embodied by Voldemort.

However, while that approach to understanding Rowling's narrative may satisfy traditional readers, in fact, such a view leads to a reductive sense of the work. For all its conventional attributes, *Harry Potter and the Sorcerer's Stone* has complexities inherent in its narrative that the programmatic response outlined above cannot begin to comprehend. Four decades ago, Claude Lévi-Strauss had already noted a significant drawback in the application to folklore of conventional cause-and-effect approaches: "The study of myths raises a methodological problem, in that it cannot be carried out according to the Cartesian principle of breaking down the difficulty into as many parts as may be necessary for finding the solution. There is no real end to mythological analysis, no hidden unity to be grasped once the breaking-down process has been completed."[14] The open-ended approach for which Lévi-Strauss calls suggests many of the attributes of chaos/complexity theory, and these ideas lead to alternative forms of reading that offer much richer interpretive options.

Heisenberg's Uncertainty Principle, stating that the act of measurement is bound to affect the attributes of the thing measured, once again provides a model for this approach. Heisenberg's scientific ideas provide metaphors that illuminate for us how habits of reading transform that which we read and thus generate multiple interpretive options in what seems to be the most prescriptive of genres. From this model, I argue that the pleasure that comes from fairy tales grows out of a reader's inclination to perceive numerous discourses within their narratives. Understanding a fairy tale is not a matter of articulating a particular interpretation. Rather, it encompasses the process of mapping the points where the narrative invites intervention (measurement) and therefore encourages the reader to reconfigure the story.

This approach means asking readers to take into account how conceptions of *Harry Potter and the Sorcerer's Stone* change after the application of interpretive methods. Though at first this description may seem to echo familiar elements of reader response or reception theory, in fact this approach offers a more radical range of options for generating meaning. It assumes that any reading, whether governed by conventional or unorthodox methods, will have the same destabilizing effect. If every reading changes the thing that is read in a unique fashion, then the text of *Harry Potter and the Sorcerer's Stone* is never the same work twice running.

Simply accepting the impact of the field theory, however, does little to expand one's appreciation of the work. Nonetheless, it does immediately highlight the drawbacks of more conventional methods. Assigning character types to Harry and the others in the story, for instance, brings out familiar associations with the fairy-tale genre. At the same time, it frustrates broader readings of the work by imposing prescriptive values on the otherwise pluralistic elements of the story. Alternative methodologies can prove just as exclusionary. Thus, finding an indictment of a materialist society within the narrative provides an interesting cultural critique, but this view also leads to limited readings by ignoring other thematic options. A genuinely less-restrictive approach sustains multiple conceptions without settling upon one. It stands as analogous to the wave/particle approach to light, which enables two contradictory theories to operate simultaneously.

Like any fairy tale worth its name, *Harry Potter and the Sorcerer's Stone* uses presumptions of goodness as a means of differentiating its characters. Harry is good, as are Hagrid, Hermione, and a number of other characters, not because of what they do but because they are associated with the dominant group in the wizard society, those attached to Hogwarts, which the narrative has identified as good. (Hogwarts itself gains an aura of goodness as much from its preeminence as from any demonstrably good trait.) Likewise, Voldemort is labeled as evil because his constant war on his fellow wizards puts him at odds with that dominant group. Others who fall into that category are seen as evil through negation; they are not good or fall short of being good.

If I attempt, however, to define the nature of goodness in *Harry Potter and the Sorcerer's Stone*, I encounter the same difficulty that crops up in many other fairy tales and that, consequently, blunts the effectiveness of conventional readings. The specific qualities that distinguish goodness from evil become difficult to discern. In *Jack and the Beanstalk*, for instance, the disobedient boy trades a cow for beans, steals from a stranger, and murders the man whom he has robbed when he is in danger of being caught, yet the fairy tale ranks Jack and not the giant (whose crimes are arguably far less egregious) as good. In the Rowling book, Harry Potter is disobedient, violates countless rules at Hogwarts (abetted by the headmaster), and deceives any number of people, yet, as in Jack's story, the narrative never questions his goodness.

Indeed, the source of the goodness that singles out Harry and others as the noble characters in the fairy tale proves to be an essential but indeterminate factor. It is the strange attractor that gives shape to the features of the fairy tale. It is the force that allows us to identify how we are meant to read the work in the conventional sense, but it is also the feature that is impossible to locate. If I contextualize goodness, seeing it as it emerges in *Harry Potter and the Sorcerer's Stone*, rather than applying more general concepts to it, the limitations of the term disappear. Instead it becomes a tool for comprehending the multiplicity of Rowling's story.

Invoking the image from chaos/complexity theory helps me understand how I come to a specific reading. I need not define or even discern goodness in terms that have validity beyond the work. Goodness becomes simply a label in *Harry Potter and the Sorcerer's Stone* that helps in the sorting of characters into different categories. It loses any inherent or universal qualities, and in consequence it undermines assumptions about the static nature of an individual's character. Identifying a character as good in the story does not prescribe our seeing goodness in the same way in a different work of literature.

Knowing that goodness acts as the attractor for various characters enables me to read with confidence in the unity and integrity of the work, and it relieves me of the burden of constructing arguments that offer moral justification for behavior that, outside the validating environment of Rowling's book, seems heinous. Further, realizing the existence of the strange attractor points up unconventionality in traditional interpretations of which I was not aware. It explains how I can overlook thematic inconsistencies to arrive at the predictable reading, and, more importantly, it points toward readings that are otherwise unavailable through conventional interpretive modes.

Positing other strange attractors also acting as unifying forces within the narrative causes even more significant interpretive variations to appear, and it realigns conceptions of characters throughout the work. If, for instance, I identified intelligence as a strange attractor, grouping certain impressions of characters and events, the hierarchy of the story would change markedly. Harry, the hero of the piece in conventional approaches, would take a backseat to Hermione, who uses her mind with greater agility and shows sharper analytic skills. Hagrid, who in a more traditional reading of *Harry Potter and the Sorcerer's Stone* stands out as a loveable and loyal if sometimes bumbling figure, would become a negative though not very significant figure who acts as an impediment to the favorable resolution of the story. Conversely, the Dursleys, who in other readings take the role of malevolent if ultimately unsuccessful impediments to Harry's development, would assume a less sinister mode simply because their stupidity absolves them from responsibility. In fact, a reading that privileges intelligence would make the Dursleys, Hagrid, and even Harry pawns to higher forces whose minds shape the events of the story.

In a clearly delineated hierarchy, the more intelligent manipulate the less intelligent for ends that those with more limited cognitive powers cannot even imagine. Since another strange attractor has already shown the relativity of goodness, I cannot redeem stupid characters by deeming them morally superior. Further, the arbitrary nature of the term *goodness* frees characters from the concern that their actions could bring about a shift in designations. Thus, the Dursleys' stubborn and unreasoned intransigence to the idea of Harry going to Hogwarts allows Hagrid, himself limited though far more acute than the Dursleys, to avoid opprobrium for his behavior even as he terrorizes them with increasingly overbearing manifestations of his power. Through Hagrid's manipulation, the Dursleys not only achieve Hagrid's goal of informing Harry of his selection by the school (a foregone conclusion), but they also impress upon Harry the significance of the honor that would provoke such a display. The narrative does not question the moral right of terrorizing creatures as limited as the Dursleys. Their stupidity bars our sympathy.

Stratification does not end here, however. Readers, no matter what their points of view, will quickly see that Hagrid's acuity is only relative and that defining levels of intelligence permeate all characterizations. This feature goes beyond the ability of Voldemort to trick Hagrid into revealing secrets that he should keep to himself. It also works to undermine the effectiveness of Ron, Harry, and Hermione, who seek to use their intelligence but who lack direction. The foolishness of Hagrid in keeping a dragon as a pet forces Harry and his friends to shift their attention from the search for the secret of the third-floor corridor to the problem of removing the unwanted beast from the school grounds. Further, Hagrid's benevolence has an additional diverting effect. Because his clumsy and ill-informed acts of kindness often require as much attention as his blunders, Hagrid's own stupidity remains a continual roadblock to sympathetic individuals, who expend energy that would otherwise be directed toward solving the tale's mystery toward protecting his feelings.

From this perspective, even Harry, touted throughout the story as the one who will act as a savior to the wizard community, performs more like a tool than an independent actor. From the moment that the letters from Hogwarts begin to arrive to the final confrontation with Voldemort, he has difficulty grasping situations. More often than not he acts according to someone else's direction. This makes his grasp of events often tentative at best. Even after his putative victory, Harry still cannot digest the implications of the complex relationship with Professor Snape, who both actively dislikes Harry and just as aggressively works to protect him.

With intelligence as the distinguishing trait, Dumbledore and Voldemort stand out as key narrative figures. They are the ones who fully understand the ramifications of the struggle in which they are engaged, and they both show consistent adeptness at using others to move their own ambitions forward. This perspective marks the seeming defeat of Voldemort at the end of the book as a false conclusion. Certainly, it singles out a stage in the intellectual struggle between two central figures. However, as is evident with Voldemort's escape from destruction, the "conclusion" reflects only a stage in the battle back and forth. In addition, this point of view realigns the stakes of the struggle; at issue is not the question of who is right or wrong but rather who is smarter.

At the same time, intelligence provides a yardstick no more stable than goodness. It too has a somewhat arbitrary quality, a trait conveyed by narrative decree rather than earned through consistent behavior. For instance, characters of supposedly high intelligence, such as Dumbledore, nonetheless fail to take all contingencies into account and thus provoke the necessary excitement of a last-minute rescue. The apparently stupid Dursleys nonetheless manage to keep Harry from any awareness of his unique background for the first ten years of his life. Stupid is as stupid does. Or, in other words, smart and stupid are left to the reader to label.

In another example, I might settle upon resistance to authority as an alternative strange attractor. This choice would underscore the subversive elements of *Harry Potter and the Sorcerer's Stone* and of course would reorder the presumed hierarchy of admirable figures. As with intelligence, recognizing the importance of rebelliousness does not change the boundaries of the story, but rather it gives a much different configuration to what occurs within the narrative.

The most striking consequence of discerning resistance to authority as a unifying characteristic is the inversion of the status of those at Hogwarts. Every member of the staff from Dumbledore on down, with the exception of Quirrell, becomes a figure worthy of disdain rather than admiration. They adhere in lockstep fashion to a system that will never be improved because they lack the courage to question it. They become complicit in all the flaws of the system because they are determined to uphold it without modification.

By the same token any number of seeming bumblers, malcontents, and troublemakers take on a new status. The Dursleys no longer appear as grotesquely selfish bumpkins. Rather, they are individuals unwilling to be cowed, at least initially, by a far more powerful force who seeks to dictate their behavior. Hagrid, despite his limited intelligence, shows a measure of distinction in his openness to bending rules and operating outside the system. And Ron and Hermione regain some of the prestige that they lost in readings focusing on other traits, for they too are determined to act according to their wills despite prohibitions laid down by the school.

The real changes come with Snape, Quirrell, Harry, and Voldemort. Snape, who seemed to be a mildly subversive character in his willingness to punish Harry and others in an arbitrary fashion, is really the most devoted to maintaining the status quo. Quirrell, who for most of the story had appeared as little more than a weak reed, in the end shows a willingness to challenge the fundamental structure of the wizard society. To a degree, Harry falls in the same category, for much of what he accomplishes during his first year at Hogwarts comes about because he subverts rules and defies authority. This makes him closer to Voldemort than to Dumbledore. Voldemort, like Satan in some readings of Milton's *Paradise Lost*, becomes from this perspective more admirable and certainly more interesting than the so-called forces of good, for he is willing to risk all for his principles, whereas the others choose to conform to the status quo. Almost any fair-minded reading would ascribe the same attitude to Harry when he subverts authority. Dumbledore, on the other hand, while willing to bend the rules on occasion, shows a far greater loyalty to traditional authority than does either Voldemort or Harry.

Single-mindedness stands out as yet another trait that could serve to unify criticisms of *Harry Potter and the Sorcerer's Stone*. By dividing characters in the story according to that trait and then judging them by their ability to meet it, we create a very different sense of the narrative. We begin to see figures distinguishing themselves by a devotion to an overriding goal rather than by dividing their attention over a range of aims.

Privileging this new strange attractor produces very sharp changes in perception. The Dursleys, if not perfect, show admirable determination that the often-vacillating Harry does not seem to possess. Professor Snape, when we gave other attractors prominence, appeared as odious as any character in the narrative. From this perspective, however, he emerges as a figure deserving respect for his unswerving commitment to a single view, though readers are misled as to what that view may be. Most significantly, Voldemort and Dumbledore emerge as the foremost characters in the story, not because of the beliefs that each espouses but rather for their unflinching determination to reframe the world according to those creeds.

That final distinction is most important, for it sets up an interpretation of *Harry Potter and the Sorcerer's Stone* that is far different from the conventional fairy-tale reading. Single-mindedness imbues an amoral dispensation on motivation. It does not matter so much what I believe as how fiercely I pursue the implications of that belief. So-called moral endings take a different turn when such a standard becomes the central guideline for interpretation.

The real significance of these points, however, is not that I can read *Harry Potter and the Sorcerer's Stone* from a range of perspectives. What figures as the crucial aspect of this approach is that the features that I can label strange attractors, and that consequently enable these different readings, coexist within the work. Goodness, intelligence, resistance to authority, single-mindedness, and countless other traits that I could highlight are always there in the narrative, though different readers will recognize them in different ways. In much the same fashion that strange attractors point to local unities within a turbulent liquid and that overall turbulence is contained within the boundaries of the fluid, these literary strange attractors show the complexities simultaneously at work in the book. That means that to choose one reading over any of the others is to adopt an approach every bit as conventional as that outlined at the beginning of this discussion.

The existence of a range of contradictory affinities (not values, for that would endow them with a stability that they do not have) has a subversive impact on readings. A moral arbitrariness allows any of a number of possible qualities to serve as the unifying abstract force in reading the story. In order to understand the implications of this condition—a subversion of the legitimacy of any presumed moral authority in the work—I must examine *Harry Potter and the Sorcerer's Stone* with all of these strange attractors operating simultaneously.

When all the forces are considered, Harry becomes a kaleidoscopic representation of contemporary culture. Various idealistic and pragmatic positions slide back and forth before a viewer's consciousness. In the end, the book offers not so much guidelines for proper living as a catalogue of the diverse forces that impede a full understanding of the metaphysical world that surrounds us.

The significant aspect of this observation is not that the narrative of *Harry Potter and the Sorcerer's Stone* moves forward with the kind of multilayered polyvocality identified by Mikhail Bakhtin. Rather, Rowling's book offers a glimpse of the contradictions inherent in ordinary (and in Harry's case extraordinary) human intercourse. This depiction of the metaphysical pluralism that produces contradictory images of the characters in Rowling's narrative may conjure up the bête noire of secular humanism, so intimidating to some thinkers in the early 1980s, but that association reduces her representations to political caricature. In fact, *Harry Potter and the Sorcerer's Stone* distances itself from prescriptive moral positioning, and instead, like the most sophisticated fairy tales, it invites the reader to respond to its antinomies by more closely examining the system that he or she employs to unify the world.

5   "I sing of arms and of a man"

The Post-Newtonian Hero

At least 999 of a thousand scientific papers are about complex details,
but the one that we treasure and for which we award a Nobel Prize is
the one that reveals a new simplicity.
JACK COHEN AND IAN STEWART

THE PUBLICATION IN 1936 of J.R.R. Tolkien's magisterial study *"Beowulf: The Monsters and the Critics"* marked a turning point in the examination of the great Old English poem. Tolkien urged readers to take what was at the time a radically new approach: to see *Beowulf* not just as a repository of unique lexical features of the earliest form of our modern language but also as a complex literary work. While paying homage to the achievements of those linguists whose studies of *Beowulf* did much to illuminate understanding of the fundamental elements of the evolution of our native tongue, Tolkien saw that work as limited, because it did not engage the poem "as a work of art."[1] Tolkien rejected efforts to categorize the poem as simply a linguistic curiosity, a glorified folktale, or a historical document and called for scholars to examine it in the same way that any other literary work would be studied.

The critical tradition that quickly grew up as a result of Tolkien's essay has unquestionably answered his call for sophisticated literary interpretations of the poem. At the same time, despite any number of thoughtful critiques, the inherent linearity of these approaches has limited their impact.[2] Since Tolkien began the process of recovering *Beowulf* as a literary work, perhaps the most common critical approach has labeled the poem as the great epic of Old English literature, and a cursory examination of what conventional critics see as its defining features shows that *Beowulf* contains all of the elements that constitute an epic.[3] It is a long narrative poem. Its discourse foregrounds the actions of a central figure, the title character, who occupies a high position in his society. And the adventures undergone by this central character act as a means of celebrating the values or behavior important to the nation or ethnic group featured in the work.[4]

Categorizing *Beowulf* in this way has given it an undeniable legitimacy. Its designation as an epic places it at the center of a literary tradition and establishes clear-cut parameters for understanding its meaning. Nonetheless, acceptance of this programmatic view of the poem as a great national epic has paved the way for prescriptive interpretive approaches that produce readings more directive and exclusionary than anyone seeking a full appreciation of *Beowulf* would wish for the poem.

This is not to say that characteristics within the poem do not support the conventional assumptions of such approaches. Narrative patterns familiar to the epic's style abound throughout the work's structure. In more than 3,000

lines, the poem details Beowulf's development from a nondescript young
man to a paragon:

> poorly regarded
> for a long time, was taken by the Geats
> for less than he was worth: and their lord too
> had never much esteemed him in the mead-hall.
> They firmly believed that he lacked force,
> that the prince was a weakling; but presently
> every affront to his deserving was reversed. (2183–89)[5]

The emblematic role of the poem's hero is always emphasized, for in highlighting Beowulf's achievements in his fights with Grendel, with Grendel's
mother, and with the dragon, the poem provides a clear catalogue of the
ideal traits for a warrior in the society that it celebrates:

> Thus Beowulf bore himself with valour;
> he was formidable in battle yet behaved with honour
> and took no advantage; never cut down
> a comrade who was drunk, kept his temper
> and, warrior that he was, watched and controlled
> his God-sent strength and his outstanding
> natural powers. (2177–83)

Further, the formulaic descriptive passages that recur over the course of
the narrative exemplify the virtues that the society in the poem esteems.
Throughout *Beowulf*, for instance, detailed descriptions in the poem provide numerous examples of the qualities that distinguish the nature of a hero
and underscore the high regard enjoyed by a man who possesses such traits:

> he would have to rely
> on the might of his arm. So must a man do
> who intends to gain enduring glory
> in a combat. Life doesn't cost him a thought. (1534–37)

Repeated elaborations of heroic characteristics that set Beowulf apart emphasize their general value within this society, even as the narrative celebrates his particular achievements.

The poem also lays out various features that inform the ethical system of
the world of the poem. In outlining the points of view and the patterns of
behavior that enable individuals to cope with life's reversals, *Beowulf* represents a society that has developed a programmatic pragmatism as a response
to the vagaries and upheavals of a violent world: "Wise sir, do not grieve. It is
always better / to avenge dear ones than to indulge in mourning" (1384–85).
At the same time, *Beowulf* repeatedly acknowledges the stabilizing force of

Christian belief—"The truth is clear: / Almighty God rules over mankind / and always has" (700–702)—even as it presents a tone of superstitious acquiescence regarding the way fate shapes human life: "So may a man not marked by fate / easily escape exile and woe / by the grace of God" (2291–93). Perhaps most emphatically, an aura of pessimism cloaks the narrative's conception of the world, generally taking the form of a feeling of foreboding that intrudes into even the most joyful of discourses: "The Shielding nation / was not yet familiar with feud and betrayal" (1017–18).

Overall, the narrative seems to be invoking an ordered, Aristotelian worldview that presumes an ability to discern causes for observable effects, whatever the specific environment in which they originate. In fact, what these conflicting invocations underscore is not a faith in a world ordered by some supernatural system but rather a sense that neither system adequately explains events in the world. What comes out in the action of the poem is a world better explained by the nonlinear values of the New Physics than by the cause-and-effect thinking of exclusionary logic popular since Aristotle's time.

As numerous scholars have already noted, highlighting these features within the poem foregrounds a complex social environment readily comprehensible to attentive readers.[6] It is this environment, full of seeming contradictions that not only coexist but form a cohesive whole, that suggests a richer interpretive field than that delineated by exclusionary either/or analyses. In stating its code of behavior, for example, *Beowulf* proposes a defense of a militant Christianity that does not turn the other cheek. Rather, it emphasizes the justification of violence when sanctioned by the family or clan. The world of the poem invites readers or listeners to engage in a profoundly fatalistic worldview without becoming paralyzed. And at the same time, it holds out the promise of an eternal reward attainable without compromising the warrior code. The moral system implied by these values presents a sophisticated response to the harsh aspects of the environment encompassed by the narrative, for it combines a determined optimism, affirming the possibility of success in any human endeavor, with an insistent fatalistic belief that the elements of a harsh material world will inevitably collaborate to end the life of the individual.

Contemporary critical approaches, such as Lacanian psychoanalysis, attempt to present more inflected views of *Beowulf* than those found in interpretations of the poem as an epic. They elaborate on the consequences of the behavior that the work seems to celebrate. At the same time, such putatively innovative readings in fact reinscribe prescriptive interpretive forms.

A good example of this appears in Janet Thormann's endeavors to examine from a Lacanian point of view the function of violence in the poem, especially as it connects to materialism.[7] Thormann attempts to contextualize *Beowulf* by positing the vivid descriptions of violence as particularly attractive to many who originally heard the poem. In her view the accounts would have been evocative of their daily experiences, and these representations would have conveyed approval of the lives led by the audience. Thormann goes on to assert that contemporary readers, while feeling ambivalence over the celebration of savagery, also can use these incidents as a guide for comprehending the ethos of the world of the medieval Danes: "That violence is valorized to be an ethical behavior, even as it is described as brutal and ugly."[8]

Savagery for Thormann goes beyond validating the nastiness of daily life. She believes that a specific form of violence, revenge, sustains equilibrium in the society of the poem and of its audience. This forwards the hypothesis that Beowulf takes on heroic dimensions for readers at least in part because he has committed himself to this culture of reciprocity embodied by, among other things, revenge. Further, the interpretive strategy of establishing violence as a tool of ethical conduct legitimizes its enjoyment by characters and audience alike. Thormann looks for legitimacy by evoking Lacan's endorsement of "transgressive enjoyment." Violence, with all its anarchic force, paradoxically serves to unify a group, and the pursuit of revenge gives cohesiveness and direction to its behavior. Indeed, from this point of view, violence structures the very society of the poem.

In an admirable fashion, Thormann's critique goes well beyond the predictable views of the poem that concentrate on its status as oral poetry, linguistic resource, or repository of folk tradition.[9] In consequence it illuminates areas often overlooked in traditional readings. At the same time, while overstepping the boundaries of conventional interpretation, this Lacanian approach ultimately succumbs to the same limitations of any mode of thought wedded to Cartesian logic. Its analysis develops along exclusionary lines that progressively narrow the interpretive scope. On its own, it cannot satisfy one's desire to engage the range of imaginative elements within *Beowulf*, because it inevitably must give precedence to one point of view over all the others.

This limitation impedes full understanding, for within the structure of the poem, other elements offer insistent alternatives to exclusionary linearity. *Beowulf* does far more than simply celebrate the life of a single hero. Although the poem offers numerous accounts of the adventures of its title character, many digressions call attention to the successes and failures of other individuals as well—Wheostan, for example, whose exploits as an exile earn him such esteem that he is honored by the uncle of a man he has slain (2609–19). Several of these accounts implicitly reject the patterns of behavior that Beowulf followed. These instances do not so much challenge the status of Beowulf as paragon as argue that he represents one of any number of alternatives—equally significant—afforded by his society. These references outline a simultaneity that Cartesian readings cannot compass.

On a more individual level, while the narrative recounts incidents throughout the life of Beowulf, it feels no chronological constraints in the ordering of that account. Whether describing an individual's ability to vanquish nature, warriors, or monsters, the narrative makes no effort to tell these stories in the order in which they occurred. This approach implicitly invites alternative conclusions regarding what activities lead to the formation of a heroic nature or, for that matter, when a particular character attains the status of hero. This condition then invites us to perceive more complexity in the dynamics of the poem's society.

Finally, at a number of points in the poem, analogous events in the lives of other warriors show that Beowulf's experiences are by no means unique. His feats in battle, his political triumphs, and his struggle to establish identity mirror the experiences of other figures commemorated in the poem. These analogues call into question whether readers should view the poem's ostensive hero as a unique individual or as the normal representation of the male figure of that society.

An unmistakable measure of circularity informing the discourse of the poem compounds this aura of multiplicity. Various speakers, including the narrator, blur the distinctions between events set in the past or future and action unfolding in the present. Someone evokes past experiences to suggest a way of understanding the present, and then boasts about what deeds he will accomplish as a way of blunting imminent threats. Indeed, the tone of most accounts shows no effort to distinguish between what has happened, what is happening, and what will happen. With this approach, the narrative measurably undermines the causal nature of specific actions by disrupting their chronological sequence.[10] At several points in the poem, recollections bring the events of a past feud into the meadhall during a time of peace and produce images of upcoming conflicts. One tragic incident seems to mimic another. Marriages provoke blood feuds that are mediated by marriages, which provoke blood feuds. Instead of describing a logical, cause-and-effect progression of actions, these accounts appear as cyclical patterns of interchangeable incidents.

Early on, the discourse manifests the importance of bringing events of the past into the present as more than a simple concern for preserving their memory. In the communal world of the poem, a character derives and retains his identity not simply by his actions but by the recollections of those actions by his society. Individuals know that existence, both during and after one's life, turns upon society's memory, and consequently they do their utmost to cultivate communal recollections, both by their actions and by their efforts to remind others of what they have already done. Beowulf's *bona fides* allude not only to the deeds he has performed but to the esteem he has earned among his own people through those efforts. Boasting of achievements brings the past into the present and commits the speaker to future action:

> So every elder and experienced councilman
> among my people supported my resolve
> to come here to you, King Hrothgar,
> because all knew of my awesome strength.
> They have seen me boltered in the blood of enemies
> when I battled and bound five beasts,
> raided a troll-nest in the night-sea
> slaughtered sea-brutes. I have suffered extremes
> and avenged the Geats (their enemies brought it
> upon themselves, I devastated them). (415–24)

It can come as no surprise that Beowulf and others relate the details of incidents like the struggle with Grendel or the death of Grendel's mother time and again (see 957–78, 1652–76, and 2069–2150). Those accounts become as much a part of their ongoing identities as the titles *doctor, judge,* or *reverend* encompass the natures of contemporary individuals.

Furthermore, such recapitulation has a dynamic effect upon identity. Just as subatomic measurements reshape that world that the scientist seeks to define, the very act of recapitulation reconfigures the deeds of the hero. Retelling breaks chronology. The accomplishments cease to be confined to a particular time or place. Instead, they assume positions as ever-present and ever-evolving parts of the hero's persona. Thus, when Beowulf evokes his fight with Grendel as, fifty years later, he prepares to fight the dragon that is devastating his kingdom (2520–21), he boasts as a way of identifying who he is and who he will be rather than as a nostalgic appeal to who he was. Memory—individual and communal—rather than physical prowess guarantees Beowulf's continuing stature as a hero, and by extension language surpasses actions as the force that establishes character. From this point of view, the scops who celebrate deeds are as important to the hero as the deeds themselves—indeed, arguably more important. Simple cause-and-effect relationships cannot in themselves define the configuration of the heroic persona. It requires the imaginative multiplicity of poets to formulate descriptions that encompass the role.

Additionally, features of the poem challenge the stability of any view that traces Beowulf's life from that of a young man to an old king. In fact, the narrative strains to overturn the impression of a unity that comes through Cartesian linearity, with one event serving as the cause of the next. Frequent digressions break this pattern and suggest instead a cyclical view of life.

When, for example, Beowulf recounts his swimming contest with Brecca (529–81), he not only brings the past into the present as a way of establishing his long-standing notoriety, but he also prefigures analogous events that will occur when he seeks out Grendel's mother under the mer. We do not see an evolution or causal development in his nature. One experience does not produce greater insight or abilities that will then come to bear on the next. Rather, from the start of the poem to its end, Beowulf, through his strength and valor, consistently demonstrates his attributes as a hero.

The narrative, however, does more than just establish analogues among the past, the present, and the future. It treats all events with a contemporaneous view that makes each period seem an ongoing presence in the world. When, for example, Beowulf has returned to the land of the Geats and is recounting his adventures in the kingdom of the Danes to Hygelac, his recollection of Hrothgar's daughter, Freawaru, leads to a poignant digression. Freawaru is betrothed to Ingeld in a match designed to bring peace between the Danes and the Heathobards. The wedding has not yet occurred, yet Beowulf imagines horrific events that will mark the wedding feast. In great detail (2031–69), Beowulf describes how "an old spearman" will rouse resentment in some young Heathobard whose father's armor is now being worn by a Dane: "Now, my friend, don't you recognize / your father's sword, his favourite weapon, / the one he wore when he went out in his war-mask / to face the Danes on that final day?" (2047–50). Beowulf foresees the tension escalating to the point of violence: "until one of the lady's retainers lies / spattered in blood, split open / on his father's account" (2059–61). Though none of these events has as yet come to pass, Beowulf describes them in the same manner as his account of his own adventures among the Danes. His sense of the structure of his society makes these descriptions of things to come as real for him and his listeners as his accounts of the events that he has already experienced.

This aspect does more than provide an aura of immediacy for every event. It disrupts our modern sense of contingency. It blunts the notions of control and individual choice, and instead insinuates an aura of inevitability. Beowulf does not live in a world that can be mastered or even modified. Rather, he exists in an environment that will present recurring challenges that he will meet only as long as fate has decreed it. This gives everything the feel of a continuous present tense, with no regard for what has occurred and no expectations for what is to come. Neither the past nor the future can influence the inevitability of events already determined by fate. Although characters move inevitably toward the outcome decreed by fate, in all instances prior to that outcome, a tremendous freedom of action and consequence obtain.

Because the poem does not restrict this sense of simultaneity to Beowulf and his friends, the significance of this condition is evident. It recurs in the words of the narrator, who seamlessly integrates a reference to the destruction of Heorot into its initial description, giving the fiery end a presence equal to any of the hall's material features: "The hall towered, / its gables wide and high and awaiting / a barbarous burning. That doom abided" (81–83). This easy discursive movement, unrestricted by chronology, makes the difference between actual and virtual events difficult to discern and suggests that from the point of view of the poem's protagonists, such a differentiation would have little significance.

Likewise, reflexivity blunts the sharp distinctions between one occurrence and another. Heroes follow patterns of behavior that echo one another's achievements. In celebrating Beowulf's defeat of Grendel, a traditional singer recounts Sigemund's exploits in slaying a dragon (883–914), in terms strikingly similar to what will take place more than fifty years in the future, when Beowulf confronts a dragon. At the feast commemorating Beowulf's victory, a minstrel tells of the Fight at Finnsburg (1070–1158), an event that has taken place and that follows much the same scenario as the account of the fight at Freawaru's wedding, mentioned above. Finally, late in the poem when Beowulf, the aged king, recollects past struggles between the Geats and the Swedes (2472–2509), he does so in language quite similar to the apocalyptic tones of the messenger who, after Beowulf's death, speaks in tones of inevitability of the upcoming wars with the Frisians and Swedes (2911–3008), seamlessly blending references to past fights with descriptions of future conflicts.

Personal feuds and national rivalries carry the same weight in terms of shaping events. Oscillation, not linearity, configures the lives of individuals in the society described by the poem. While names and locations of specific events may change, the patterns that they follow do not. Recurrence wears away the common linear distinctions between past, present, and future, and the cycle of repetition takes on as much significance within the poem as the seemingly evolving story of Beowulf. When the narrative mentions the unfortunate reign of Heremod (1709–22) or the egregious behavior of Queen Modthryth (1931–57), it is not simply recalling history in interesting digressions. It is reminding listeners of the human tendencies that lurk always within their society and that reassert themselves with a regularity that belies the notion of a world experiencing any sort of causal, linear development. In consequence, these allusions describe the ethos of the world of the poem as precisely as any account of Beowulf's achievements.

More elements than recurrent patterns of human behavior, however, shape events in the world of the poem, and this is where attentiveness to nonlinearity heightens our conceptions of what transpires. Like Lorenz's butterfly influencing the weather in Texas, seemingly trivial acts recounted in the narrative can and do have a significant impact on incidents throughout the poem. A single word or phrase can produce mayhem or restore order. A warrior's choice of the garments that he will wear to a particular feast can alter the likelihood of peace or war between two peoples. A moment's carelessness by a slave causes a lord's displeasure, which goads the slave to seek propitiation by stealing a single cup from a treasure hoard. The rage of the dragon guarding the hoard finds outlet in the attack on Geatish society. And the death of Beowulf while fending off that attack leads to the destruction of the nation he endeavored to safeguard. Time and again the narrative of *Beowulf* gives examples of a system extremely sensitive to slight changes in initial conditions.

On top of this, people within the poem feel at best only a tangential control over the events in their lives. Fate always has the dominant role in the way events unfold, but the poem also sets up a complex relationship between it and the individual. Beowulf acknowledges this connection early in the narrative, even as he celebrates the life of a man of courage: "Often, for undaunted courage, / fate spares the man it has not already marked" (572–73).

Additionally, repeated acknowledgment of the shaping power of divine will further circumscribes, without completely dictating, individual freedom of action: "holy God / decided the victory. It was easy for the Lord, / the Ruler of Heaven, to redress the balance / once Beowulf got back up on his feet" (1553–56). Throughout the poem Christianity serves as a force that may fluctuate in prominence but that consistently contributes to the shape of events. What stands in greater significance than the amount of influence exerted by either fate or divine will is the way that together they realign perceptions within the world of the poem. These elements create an ethos that supercedes the limits laid down by a Newtonian, cause-and-effect universe open to comprehension through understanding the function of all its parts. Instead, they delineate the features of an environment full of unpredictable forces, like Grendel, that simply appear and wreak havoc. Instead of a realm of periodic development, the world is subject to abrupt and often violent change.

This is not an anarchic society, however. Even with the impact exerted by fate and divine will, a cyclical inevitability conditions a great deal of the action, making the rise and fall of individuals and of nations a matter of course. Late in the poem, for instance, the messenger who informs the Geats of Beowulf's death also speculates on the destruction of their community as if it were a foregone conclusion: "So this bad blood between us and the Swedes, / this vicious feud, I am convinced, / is bound to revive: they will cross our borders / and attack in force when they find out / that Beowulf is dead" (2999–3003). This fatalism leads to the view that, rather than individual prowess, a sense of randomness, often designated as fate, ultimately determines an individual's success or failure:

> Often when one man follows his own will
> many are hurt. This happened to us.
> Nothing we advised could even convince
> the prince we loved, our land's guardian,
> not to vex the custodian of the gold (3077–81)
>
> . . . .
>
> The hoard is laid bare,
> but at a grave cost; it was too cruel a fate
> that forced the king to that encounter. (3084–86)

Through all of this, the narrative underscores not the anarchic but the arbitrary condition that informs the lives of characters, further eroding the significance of an individual's actions. Thus, when Beowulf's hubris causes him to eschew weapons in facing Grendel (676–81), rather than putting his life at great risk, he unwittingly adopts the only strategy that would defeat the monster, for "no blade on earth, no blacksmith's art / could ever damage their demon opponent" (801–2). All this suggests a narrative structure different from what most of the conventional readings of the poem have discerned, one in which events occur as much fortuitously as through the efforts of the hero. Indeed, the epithet *hero* and the general sense of the poem as an embodiment of epic virtues become more ambiguous if individual successes are based at least as much upon chance as upon one's own efforts.

If epic conventions do not apply, then neither do epic conclusions. In a traditional epic reading, the central character is an ideal hero. In more sophisticated readings, critics would qualify or find exceptions to that ideal, but in conventional approaches shaped by Cartesian thinking, the overall impression of the paragon remains. When we move from the linearity of a Newtonian system to the divergence of post-Einsteinian thinking, the constrictions of either/or exclusivity disappear. That is to say, by the narrative's own admission, Beowulf's success comes as much through fate and divine will as through his own nature. Therefore, the centrality of his role as a model of behavior must be called into question. Once emphasis shifts from Beowulf as the defining force of the narrative, a range of other interpretive possibilities emerges.

The elements already highlighted demonstrate that within the narrative of *Beowulf* less structure and less inevitability exist than critics have formerly found. The randomness discernible in much of the action gives the title character much less control over events than conventional readings have assumed and consequently diminishes his role as a paragon. He does not shape his life to conform to a particular ideal, although he certainly wishes to do so. Rather, events over which he has little or no control simply unfold. At best his approach is reactionary, and even then the results that it produces remain contingent upon forces completely removed from Beowulf's control.

Not simply actions but also evaluations take on an aura of mystery for contemporary readers. Values expressed throughout the poem have an alien and even arbitrary quality to them. Blood feuds, for instance, stand as phenomena distant from our day-to-day lives and operate in a fashion most difficult to comprehend. Nevertheless, they stand as both common and highly stylized features of Beowulf's world. Warriors show a passionate commitment to pursuing them, yet they remain tightly governed by material concerns. Thus, after a long discourse on events, Hrothgar explains, in an almost abrupt tone, how he settled the conflict between Beowulf's father, Ecgtheow, and the Wulfings: "I healed the feud by paying" (470).

Likewise, bragging, at least as practiced by Beowulf and others in the poem, stand as a custom alien to most modern sensibilities. We do not feel comfortable speaking with such self-aggrandizing tones, yet self-promotion becomes central to the identity of characters in the poem. It serves as a way of establishing presence and of reminding others of their status in relation to the speaker. Beowulf's boast before facing the dragon sums up this attitude: "I marched ahead of [Hygelac], always there / at the front of the line; and I shall fight like that / for as long as I live, as long as this sword / shall last, which has stood me in good stead / late and soon, ever since I killed / Dayraven the Frank in front of the two armies" (2497–2502).

Human relationships in the poem also take on different constructions from what modern readers might assume. For instance, Unferth offers a sword to Beowulf to assist in fighting Grendel's mother. It seems an openhanded gesture that we would applaud as generous support for a friend. The narrative, however, emphasizes another perspective, focusing upon Unferth's unwillingness to undertake the task, and judges the act as a reflection of his missing an opportunity to gain fame and renown. At the same time, we cannot understand actions by simply inverting our standards for behavior. When, in the closing lines of the poem, Wiglaf demonstrates his loyalty to Beowulf, the young man manifests an unambiguously admirable position that anyone would easily understand and endorse.

In short, many of the values advanced by the narrative of the poem stand distinct from those that obtain in modern society, even as a number of attitudes strike a familiar chord. This gives readers greater freedom in constructing the nature of Beowulf. We need not feel bound to apply the same criteria in judging Beowulf that we would to a contemporary individual nor feel obliged to invoke only the standards clearly associated with his world. Rather, the contrasts invite us to view Beowulf without imposing a prescriptive paradigm from either era.

All this suggests alternatives to an approach that foregrounds Beowulf as the interpretive fulcrum of the poem, but simply finding another pivotal figure can lead to oversimplification. That is not to diminish the importance of individuality but rather to suggest that an amalgamation of figures, strange attractors, provide the poem with a cohesion and a structure not immediately apparent to readers pursuing conventional interpretive methods. More than thirty years ago, the novelist John Gardner presented a striking alternative to traditional views of the poem, when he wrote *Grendel*, the Beowulf story from the monster's perspective.

In many ways, the Gardner novel embodies what I am suggesting is accessible from a different approach to the poem. *Grendel* humanizes the central characters of the narrative (without making them more humane) by offering more complex motivations for their behavior. Elaborating upon each figure also enables Gardner to break from depictions of types and to bring individuality to the foreground. Seeing the world from the monster's point of view makes the ethical system of the Danes and the Geats much more subjective and open to challenge. All in all, Gardner's fiction quite successfully breaks down the predictable responses to the poem that the epic conventions dictate.

Nonetheless, while Gardner's depictions show ingenuity and wit, they still suffer from the disadvantage of following linear, cause-and-effect thinking in their assessments of the world of monsters and heroes. By simply inverting the established perspective and retelling the story from the eyes of another character, Gardner is in fact giving the same overview as the original, only with different features highlighted.

Though Beowulf may seem to stand as an individual emblematic of the ideals of the poem's world, another type insistently intrudes into the narrative: the Last Survivor. Unlike the hero, a type responsible for manifesting a single function or trait, this figure takes on a more complex role. Analogous to the hero, the Last Survivor demonstrates the power of the individual to succeed, or at least to endure, in the face of tremendous hostility. At the same time, the Last Survivor also signifies an additional range of complex attitudes. He embodies the fear of isolation that permeates a tightly knit communal society whose continued existence is always threatened by harsh external forces: "My own people / have been ruined in war; one by one / they went down to death, looked their last / on sweet life in the hall" (2249–52). The Last Survivor stands for the continuity between past, present, and future, the sole chance for sustaining the identity of a particular group beyond its physical existence, yet he realizes the hopelessness of this task: "I am left with nobody / to bear a sword or burnish plated goblets" (2252–53). He reflects loyalty to a society that no longer endures, and in doing so the Last Survivor demonstrates the tenuousness of all identity in a world where few individuals possess the strength to stand alone: "Pillage and slaughter / have emptied the earth of entire peoples" (2265–66).

The poem presents this image most poignantly in the figure of the individual who buries the treasure hoard (2245) that will be guarded by the dragon who brings about Beowulf's death, but he stands as only one in a line of similar figures to whom the poem alludes. The death of the Geat King Hygelac in Friesland (2355) and the subsequent killing of his heir, Heardred, by the Swedes (2387) put Beowulf in the position of the Last Survivor. Though the Geatish people still exist, the poem clearly identifies Beowulf as the last one able to lead, and, as such, his ascension to power in fact signals the end of that society. An even more powerful representation of that image of entropy emerges as Beowulf, as an old king, recalls a tragic event from his youth, when King Hrethel's son Haethcyn accidentally killed his brother Herebeald (2430–40). Because the normal laws for taking revenge present the conflict of killing one's own child, Hrethel has no course of action open to him that will relieve his grief. In the end, the sorrow isolates and overwhelms him: "Alone with his longing, he lies down on his bed / and sings a lament; everything seems too large, / the steadings and the fields" (2460–62).

In each of these situations a single feature remains constant. The normal pattern of the succession of leaders has been disrupted, and the preservation of the society is called into question as a consequence. One individual remains to testify to the destruction of his people. As noted earlier, the cyclical application of events makes it less significant whether this event is an actual recollection or speculation of impending turmoil.

Such passages foreground the diversity of the concepts that anchor meaning within the poem. As we become more and more aware of this condition, the character of Beowulf, while still retaining significance for any reading, loses hegemony over the way we interpret the narrative. Allusions to the Last Survivor underscore the complexity of attitudes that form the community of the poem and demonstrate stark alternatives to the picture of the heroic paragon as the unifying figure of the work.

Further, the representations of fate and of divine will raise additional questions about readings of the events recounted. As evident from the narrative, the figures celebrated by the poem have only a tenuous control over their lives. Indeed, we can push the concept toward a post-Modern view of a world in which actions stand at best as arbitrary, and in the end prove meaningless, for frequent demonstrations of pessimism punctuate the poem and would seem to endorse this view. In praising the generosity of Beowulf, for example, the narrative seemingly cannot resist introducing references to antithetical behavior: "Beowulf bestowed four bay steeds / to go with the armour, swift gallopers, / all alike. So ought a kinsman act, / instead of plotting and planning in secret / to bring people to grief, or conspiring to arrange / the death of comrades" (2164–69). The complexity already noted in the construction of *Beowulf* threatens to make it an anti-epic, a chronicle not of ideals of a particular society but rather a bitter acknowledgment of its helplessness.

Certainly, a Cartesian frame of mind, seeking to trace the cause-and-effect pattern of action within the narrative, could logically lead to such a pessimistic reading. At the same time, as I have advocated throughout this study, alternative forms of reasoning can lead to a far different impression of the world of *Beowulf*. As noted above, a number of features at work in the narrative not only show the ethos of the poem as far more complex than the simple celebration of heroic values. They also underscore inherent unities that provide a sense of meaning and direction in what might seem an arbitrary and pointless world.

I have already spoken of strange attractors that give coherence to the action of the poem. The concepts of fate and divine will fall into this category. While invoking the image of the strange attractor may seem to rob individuals of their ability to act freely, a closer scrutiny of its characteristics reveals more complex functions for the concepts that manifest this ambiguous force. Fate, though seemingly programmatic, behaves with a fluidity that frustrates Cartesian predictability. It can serve as a nemesis punishing hubris: "Fate swept him away / because of his proud need to provoke / a feud with the Frisians" (1205–7). Likewise, as noted, fate can extend life based upon individual merit. Additionally, divine will can shape the results of an encounter: "It was hard fought, a desperate affair / that could have gone badly; if God had not helped me" (1656–57).

In these instances elements within the poem do two things. They affirm an ordered plan to the universe; a higher force has organized and shaped characters' lives. They also signal a degree of flexibility in the way each life plays out; a warrior can avert or bring on disaster, depending upon his demeanor. These lines testify to a world that is anything but arbitrary, and they also affirm the possibility of an individual's asserting some control over his or her destiny.

In *Beowulf* characters may not fully control events, and they may not completely understand them. Nonetheless, like the liquid in a turbulent system, they remain subject to a kind of order, and this order stands as readily discernible for a sensitive reader, even if—as with turbulence—the features of the controlling force do not completely emerge. At the end of the poem, Wiglaf, the one retainer who remained at Beowulf's side in fighting the dragon, shows that he understands what society expects from him and that he is well aware of the consequences that result when individuals fail to meet such expectations. In berating those who fled, Wiglaf speaks not merely of punishments for them but, more significantly, of punishments that will fall upon the entire society because of the failure of these men to sustain the order of behavior: "Everyone of you / with freeholds of land, our whole nation, / will be dispossessed, once princes from beyond / get tidings of how you turned and fled / and disgraced yourselves" (2886–90).

Certainly, these lines can be read as a tragic lament, but at the same time they do not sound a note of despair. The world does not change capriciously, but rather it alters because individuals have not adhered to its system. What has occurred in Beowulf's kingdom becomes a tragedy because it could have been averted. Wiglaf fully understands how events will unfold, and that, in itself, stands as a triumph. It shows his faith in the existence of order when there is so much evidence to support the view of an anarchic world.

The consequences of this way of viewing the poem give it a kind of complexity familiar in quantum physics. That is to say, understanding comes not as a deconstruction of the poem but rather through an expansion of the assumptions of linearity. Beowulf's society does not stand wholly subject to exclusionary Newtonian laws, and the poem does not reflect simply a celebration of Anglo-Saxon values. At the same time, the inefficacy of the Newtonian system does not lead to the existential chaos of a nihilistic world. Rather, it evokes the features of a complex society—more complex than moderns may initially suppose—that has evolved sophisticated means for coping with conditions it cannot fully understand.

Seeing that multiplicity allows modern readers to comprehend to some degree the pluralism of the medieval world that the poem captures. Beowulf traces an environment every bit as complex as ours, and, more importantly, it recovers a tone every bit as sophisticated as that which characterizes modern society. Just as it would be foolish to presume that we understand the world of those who wrote Beowulf simply by reading the poem, it would be equally foolish to presume that a stable world exists within the poem for us to perceive. We can, however, feel that we understand the level of complexity that informed that world, and in consequence see within the poem a great deal more of interest.

6 **"A time for every purpose under heaven"**

The Circularity of Biblical Hermeneutics in the Book of Job

Physics does not study the universe but rather our knowledge about the universe.
MAX PLANCK

BECAUSE OF ITS ROLE as a metaphoric source and also as a thematic inspiration for countless Western thinkers, the Bible demands the full intellectual attention of anyone studying the imaginative responses made to literature. At the same time, a reader cannot presume to discern objective lessons —moral, cultural, or historical—from passages in the Bible. Its narrative endorses too many contrasting discourses, and its imagery supports too many diverse points of view for a common interpretation to emerge.

At the most fundamental level, conflicting perceptions of what constitutes the Bible complicate one's perceptions. Competing systems of belief vying for primacy ensure that the very scope of the term *Bible* becomes a freighted choice. The Holy Scriptures, or Tanakh, for Jews by and large consist of writings that Christian religions have labeled the "Old Testament." This distinguishes them from writings relating to the life and teachings of Jesus, which Christians call the "New Testament." Further, various Christian sects differ over the number and even order of books that make up the sacred text.[1]

Scripture's dynamic role in our culture further complicates its examination. The Bible exerts an undeniable influence as literature of faith, yet at the same time it serves a key function in both artistic and social areas. Readers seeking to apply the protocols of one point of view find themselves never completely free from the other. In particular, nontheologians with exegetic goals outside the realm of religious study face the problem of finding a way to treat whatever biblical elements they encounter in an aesthetic context as literature without giving offense to religious traditions and aspects of conviction. Certainly, the critic need not share the faith of adherents to offer a literary interpretation of the Scriptures. Nonetheless any public criticism requires keen sensitivity to the religious beliefs that the Bible represents.

Common sense affirms this approach. It would be ludicrous to attempt to deny the shaping force of images and ideas from the Bible on our conception of the world that we inhabit. Accounts of the fall from grace in the Garden of Eden, the purgation of the world through the Great Flood, the triumph of right over might in the confrontation of David and Goliath, and numerous admonitions from the words of Christ—for example, "Turn the other cheek" or "Let him who is without sin cast the first stone"—have become markers of cultural constructions and systems of values that extend beyond the specific religious dogmas expressed in the New and Old Testaments. The Bible codifies an ethical perspective that resonates across creeds to sum up values for our culture. No matter what one's individual beliefs may be, the moral precepts articulated in the Bible—the Ten Commandments, the Wisdom literature, the parables of Christ, the Sermon on the Mount, and numerous other passages from the Sacred Scripture—have come to form the basic protocols for interaction in Western society.

This means that, even in an academic environment sheltered from the influence of religion, no discussion of the Bible can disregard its moral force and still claim to be a comprehensive assessment. As the source of the social contract for private and public behavior, the teachings of the Bible lay down the rhythm of everyday life. We need not identify the prohibitions against certain forms of behavior as sins to see that the dishonesty, violence, and self-indulgence that they condemn are antisocial acts. Nor need we label other acts as virtues in order to recognize charity, probity, temperance, and self-sacrifice as traits that ennoble any individual. Because of the force of Judeo-Christian tradition on our society, any assessment of human behavior in a work of literature will turn to these tenets, drawn from lessons from the Bible, as yardsticks that reveal how our culture understands and judges character.

With this acknowledgment of the Bible's influence oscillating between aesthetic and spiritual poles, the ability to read it in a nonexclusionary fashion emerges as a crucial feature for a full aesthetic appreciation of the work. To approach accounts in the Bible with a determination to ignore their ethical resonances stands as a willful reductiveness. At the same time, allowing specific theological beliefs (or nonbeliefs) to inform readings succumbs to narrow didacticism. As with other interpretive responses outlined in this study, the ability to sustain contradictions facilitates the fullest comprehension of the work.

My efforts to apply to the Bible the interpretive approaches of this study attempt to respect its diverse roles without privileging one over another. Rather, I aim to reference scriptural writings as important features in the formation of a Western consciousness. I find the moral weight of these works undeniable, yet I hope to focus on that condition without engaging the theological differences that divisions within the Bible—and, indeed, that various versions of the Bible—promote.

Any aesthetic understanding of passages in the Bible requires recognition of their imaginative impact on our lives equal to the moral force that they exert. Undeniably, through their reiteration of values crucial to Judeo-Christian belief, accounts in the Bible give any reader, whatever his or her faith, the vocabulary needed to articulate a sense of an individual's worth, but they do much more than that. As I engage the system of metaphors that serve as the source for the imagery of Western literature, I see biblical mythology providing ethical continuity both for the efforts of writers to create vivid descriptions and of readers to comprehend them. Images of the expulsion from paradise, the destruction of human wickedness by the forces of nature, the sacrifice of an individual life for the redemption of the community, and countless other forms resonate back and forth between works of Western literature and biblical sources.

Beyond these moral concerns, for many readers the Bible stands as the only account they have encountered of life in southwestern Asia in the two millennia before the birth of Christ. Indeed, a long tradition of analyses of this work exists because it enjoys widespread popularity as a literary, historical, and anthropological resource as well as a religious document. Of course, despite its influence on the perceptions that many hold of life in the Iron Age Middle East and beyond, the Bible was not written as if it were a historical record, and it should not be read and certainly not critiqued as if it were. Its composers and compilers aimed at constructing a theological document, albeit one written with an awareness of selected historical figures, places, and events that embodied various concepts of that theology. As Northrop Frye has noted, in a work that can serve as a model for a judicious, respectful treatment of the Bible: "The Bible will only confuse and exasperate a historian who tries to treat it as history."[2]

What we need to keep in mind is that it occupies a place in our culture more diverse and more adaptable than we would expect from a typical religious work. The Bible functions as a complex social document. Unlike the mythologies represented in the works of Homer or Virgil, the stories of the Bible resonate in the imaginations of many readers with an immediacy that *The Iliad, The Odyssey,* or *The Aeneid* can never match. In a very real way it demonstrates an effort to appropriate and even to configure materialist accounts from the past to confirm metaphysical perceptions held in the present.

Even more specifically, theological protocols for biblical interpretation have had a pronounced effect upon hermeneutical methods used to understand secular works. Indeed, contemporary literary criticism derives its inclination to privilege definitive meaning to the strong influence of biblical exegesis. That practice examines the Old and New Testaments for revelations of the will of God and then attempts to articulate those revelations in language that makes the divine purpose accessible to all humans.

Such methods, however, can have reductivist consequences both for aesthetic and spiritual understanding. From the Enlightenment onward, readers have applied this exegetical tradition to an epistemological approach to literature: a search for meaning based upon the assumption that literature provides insights for a better understanding of the individual and of the world that he or she inhabits.[3] This concept follows a Cartesian model. It sees a fundamental, discernible truth inherent in any truly great literary work, and it believes that the conscientious critic can exhume that truth by coming to an understanding of the work's constituent parts.

In this fashion, literature assumes a role analogous to that of philosophy or theology. By extension, literary criticism then becomes a discipline that foregrounds metaphoric and metonymic imagery in seeking to teach us how to be better people or at the very least how to have a better sense of the world. This approach leads to the assumption that methodologies designed to reveal theological truths can also function to illuminate literary insights. (Of course, philosophy and theology also employ metaphor and metonymy. In the perspective of traditional criticism, the emphasis on the aesthetic pleasure derived from metaphor and metonymy sets literature apart from these other disciplines.)

The danger of oversimplification comes when the studied ambiguities and even blatant contradictions in many passages of the Bible raise daunting challenges to the traditional approach to the work that is the source of the exegetic methods outlined by Palmer and others. Specifically, anyone seeking to apply to examinations of the Bible the exclusionary, linear approach of Cartesian cause-and-effect thinking, particularly if the reader characterizes the Bible as a unified document, must continually decide what to suppress, what to elide, and what to ignore within an array of narrative digressions and discursions. In fact, the authors of the Bible seemingly take delight in the non sequiturs imbedded in its descriptions, the contradictions within its discourse, and the out-and-out reversals of its narrative direction. As Samuel Beckett has wryly noted in an exchange near the opening of *Waiting for Godot*, this condition has led to interpretive dilemmas at the most fundamental levels of comprehension:

VLADIMIR: Two thieves, crucified at the same time as Our Saviour. One—

ESTRAGON: Our what?

VLADIMIR: Our Savior. Two thieves. One is supposed to have been saved and the other . . . (*he searches for the contrary of saved*) . . . damned.

ESTRAGON: Saved from what?

VLADIMIR: Hell.

ESTRAGON: I'm going.

He does not move.

VLADIMIR: And yet . . . (*pause*) . . . how is it—this is not boring you I hope—how is it that of the four Evangelists only one speaks of a thief being saved. The four of them were there—or thereabouts—and only one speaks of a thief being saved. (*Pause.*) Come on, Gogo, return the ball, can't you, once in a way?

ESTRAGON: (*with exaggerated enthusiasm*). I find this really most extraordinarily interesting

VLADIMIR: One out of four. Of the other three two don't mention any thieves at all and the third says that both of them abused him.

ESTRAGON: Who?

VLADIMIR: What?

ESTRAGON: What's all this about? Abused who?

VLADIMIR: The Saviour.

ESTRAGON: Why?

VLADIMIR: Because he wouldn't save them.

ESTRAGON: From hell?

VLADIMIR: Imbecile! From death.

ESTRAGON: I thought you said hell.

VLADIMIR: From death, from death.

ESTRAGON: Well what of it?

VLADIMIR: Then the two of them must have been damned.

ESTRAGON: And why not?

VLADIMIR: But one of the four says that one of the two was saved.

ESTRAGON: Well? They don't agree and that's all there is to it.

VLADIMIR: But all four were there. And only one speaks of a thief being saved. Why believe him rather than the others?

ESTRAGON: Who believes him?

VLADIMIR: Everybody. It's the only version they know.

ESTRAGON: People are bloody ignorant apes.[4]

While Estragon's assessment of humanity may have a succinctness that appeals to enthusiastic theater audiences, it does little to resolve the conundrum facing those who wish to find a linear interpretive consistency in the four Evangelists' various representations of the death of Christ. (In fact, the situation is more confused than Vladimir remembers, for not one but two of the Gospels—Matthew 27:44 and Mark 15:32—claim that both thieves revile Christ, one—John—says nothing, and only one—Luke 24:39–43—tells the story of the Good Thief.)

The Bible does not confine such irregularities to isolated instances. From accounts of the creation of the world—told in the first chapter of Genesis and then retold in a slightly different manner in the second—onward, the Bible continuously resists the delimiting classification and the impulse toward consistency that characterize traditional criticisms informed by Cartesian thinking. Throughout the Bible, the diegetic structure frustrates exclusionary approaches. Its narratives privilege pluralism over specificity and open-endedness over closure. Thus, although traditional biblical exegesis has followed a Newtonian pattern of noting either/or causality, the text itself repeatedly demonstrates a rugged resistance to this form of classification. In particular, the Book of Job stands as a paradigm for the multiplicity of which I speak, yet it remains a popular work for both believers and nonbelievers.[5]

Like the figure of the Good Thief, who, in the last moments of his life, testifies to the redemptive power of Christ, Job as the model of humble acquiescence to mysterious and seemingly unjust torment stands out in the minds of many readers, although the details of the actual story often remain a matter of little concern. The clichéd phrase "the patience of Job" excites instant recognition by almost anyone who hears it, yet the term generally evokes a picture of long-suffering, uncomplaining endurance that in fact oversimplifies and even contradicts the complexities of the biblical account. Even more-expansive efforts to translate the story for a contemporary audience, like the Archibald MacLeish play *J.B.*, often further dilute the central concerns.[6]

Arguably, traditional biblical exegesis has contributed to reductive literary views. Given the avowed intention of finding in scriptural accounts demonstrations of the caring relationship between God and humanity, an inevitable single-mindedness informs most responses to the story of Job's sufferings. For readers concerned with articulating an aesthetic rather than the theological interpretation of Job—and therefore operating without the imperative to derive a single exclusionary reading—it remains a challenge to find an approach to reading the story that accommodates its range of seeming contradictions. A summary of the narrative shows the problematic nature of a linear, Cartesian analysis.

The Book of Job begins with the debate in heaven over the righteousness of Job. God agrees to allow Satan to test "the upright man," and the narrative quickly describes Job's loss of material possessions, children, and health. Though he refuses to curse God, Job does express regret that he was ever born. Over the couse of Job's suffering, three comforters—Bildad, Eliphaz, and Zophar—appear, and in a series of exchanges with Job, they articulate the view that God would never allow a just man to suffer in such a fashion. They each encourage Job to confess his sins and to beg forgiveness. Job rebukes each in turn. He wonders aloud why God permits him to endure such pain, and he rejects the view that only evil men face the sort of physical and emotional suffering that he has experienced.

Through all this Job remains acutely aware of his vulnerability. While admitting the foolishness of trying to stand against God, Job nonetheless challenges God to make known whatever faults of Job's have provoked such suffering. In the face of Job's adamant refusal to accept responsibility for his own suffering, his comforters eventually fall silent.

At this point, a younger man, Elihu, declaring that the inspiration of God has moved him, speaks out. He expresses anger at the comforters for giving up the argument and in essence admitting that God might be unjust. Elihu also rebukes Job for appearing to think himself right and God wrong and for demanding a reply from God. Elihu asserts that God does punish evil men, and he urges Job to stand in awe of God's powers. Job does not respond, and the impact of Elihu's diatribe remains unclear.

Then God speaks, not addressing the central question posed by Job throughout the narrative—why does He allow innocent people to suffer?—

but instead cataloguing the wonders of creation and reminding Job of his ignorance of all the mysteries of the physical world. When God asks Job if he has anything to say, Job replies that his words have been frivolous. After chastising Job for challenging His will, God continues to speak of the marvels of His creation. Job acknowledges that God is all powerful and retracts all he has said. God then rebukes the comforters for not speaking truthfully, as had Job, and commands them to make sacrifice to Him with Job acting as their intermediary. Finally, God restores Job's fortunes, and the narrative comes to an end.

Traditional readings of the Book of Job operate under a drive for reconciliation of apparent antinomies. No matter how diverse the elements inhabiting the narrative, conventional exegesis time and again follows a linear path toward isolating the central elements shaping the narrative in a search for an explanation of the suffering experienced by the book's protagonist.[7] Readers seeking religious inspiration from the story emphasize its movement from despair to hope. The account of the nearly unendurable suffering of Job assaults our senses, tempting us to see some wisdom in the bitter advice given early on to Job by his wife: "Curse God, and die" (2:20). However, in the reinstatement of Job at the end of the book—"Yahweh restored Job's fortunes, because he prayed for his friends" (42:10)—people of faith can discover a brief but consoling moment of encouragement that moves readers from despair at unfathomable suffering to hope of eventual release.

Alternately, linear views of Job provide as much satisfaction for atheists as for theists. Time and again, existentialists cite the story of Job as a marvelous illustration of the meaninglessness of life. Job stands as a figure ever subject to the whims of the forces outside of his control or even comprehension, and his sufferings call to mind Gloucester's bitter denunciation of the vulnerability of mere mortals: "As flies to wanton boys, Are we to the gods. / They kill us for their sport" (*King Lear*, IV.i.36–37). Job's restoration at the end of the book, a further demonstration of this arbitrary element in life, seems every bit as capricious as his fall in the beginning. The very lack of provocation makes Job's condition fully comprehensible for existentialists.

For either approach to work, however, the reader must impose an interpretive leveling that leaves significant contradictions unresolved. The search for a Cartesian explanation for the cause of Job's suffering simply cannot accommodate all of the narrative variations. Meir Sternberg, an articulate and thoughtful proponent of conventional modes of reading, outlines these difficulties quite clearly:

> The clash between Job's epithetic and dramatic characterizations threatens the unity of his character and lends some color to the friends' (and Satan's) insinuation that the upright Job is little more than the public image exposed by adversity. But if they are right, what are we to make of the narrator's comment about the

Sternberg's critical instincts will not allow him to leave this problem unresolved, and he goes on to discern unity in the narrative:

> Only with God's approval of Job toward the end is the apparent contradiction resolved as an extension of the initial portrait: the dramatic disclosures form a whole with their antecedents within an unsuspected, because deliberately gapped, complexity of character and world view alike. Moral perfection no longer subsumes but opposes unquestioning acceptance.[9]

A close reading of this response, however, finds Sternberg's elucidation resting on a genuine and not just an apparent contradiction. Sternberg claims that Job's restoration at the end validates his position throughout the episode, which insistently questions the reasons for his suffering. That is all well and good, but if Job is right to interrogate God, it begs the question of where God stands for failing to respond. Either Job is righteous for exposing God's injustice, or he is righteous for asking a pointless question. It also raises the issue of why the comforters and not Elihu, who takes up the same points, are punished. In either instance the argument based on cause-and-effect logic falters.

Sternberg does not stand alone in struggling with the contradictory elements that jostle for attention in the Book of Job. Many sophisticated readers have had difficulty dealing with the resistance to closure inherent in the narrative of Job. The story, beginning with the colloquy in heaven, seems structured along conventional cause-and-effect lines and appears to demonstrate how the upright man's constant faith ultimately wins for him the material comfort temporarily lost. A closer examination, however, shows a determined resistance to this traditional form of reasoning. Job's sufferings stem from nothing more than a disagreement in heaven. The concern that Job, his wife, and his comforters voice over why he must suffer is never satisfactorily addressed by God or by anyone else. The seeming acquiescence of Job to God's will appears to be little more than capitulation in the face of greater physical strength. The humbling of Job's comforters by God comes about without any real motivation, and the restoration of Job's fortunes appears as capricious as the sufferings imposed upon him at the start of the narrative. In the final analysis the contradictions that run through the book remain intact, despite conventional explicators' best efforts to resolve or, failing that, to ignore them.

Job's structure begs for alternative approaches for discerning meaning, and a series of essays offering a critique of Job from a feminist perspective provides a useful measure of the value of a nontraditional point of view.[10]

Lyn M. Bechtel, in her application of a feminist hermeneutics to Job, goes much further than most scholars in offering an alternative point of view. Referencing concepts of chaos and complexity as the basis for an alternative way of thinking, she critiques conventional approaches as insufficiently flexible to accommodate an accurate view of what the Book of Job represents. Instead, Bechtel argues that if a reader adopts a feminist paradigm for interpreting Job, that reader will perceive the "differentiated unity" that informs the narrative.

Although Bechtel does not refer specifically to Cartesian thinking, she clearly feels that the dominant "deuteronomic theology" operates in a constricted mode of perception that her own views avoid:

> [T]hese insights gleaned from modern science and ancient myth [relating to goddess theology] are nowhere to be found within modern Judaeo-Christian (patriarchal) theology, where there is no feminine dimension to the divine. Instead there is only a masculine God who transcends creation and controls it absolutely. This theology of an all-controlling God is grounded on the principles of deuteronomic theology, which tends to create an unrealistic vision of God and God's dealing with creation. In contrast, the theology behind the book of Job has incorporated the basic insights of the myth of the goddess into its version of Yahwism (although without the goddess) and has challenged the validity of deuteronomic theology.[11]

To support this concept, Bechtel invokes metaphors from the physics of Heisenberg and Einstein. She argues that at the subatomic level all entities are composed of the same matter. Thus, even when confronted with conditions apparently in complete opposition, a sameness or unity runs through all things.[12]

While this interpretation represents a promising start, in the end Bechtel's own desire for closure asserts itself. She does not pursue the implications of post-Einsteinian thinking beyond advocating sensitivity to duality. Instead she uses duality to provide the logic for replacing one linear system with another. She argues that despite the seeming hegemony of patriarchal views in Job, a reader can find clear instances supporting an alternative perspective: "The book's theology of divine randomness ultimately conforms, to a large extent, with extant strands of ancient goddess theology. The unity of oppositions, and lack of aspiration for exclusive control, are hallmarks of contemporary feminist theology too."[13] Bechtel finds instances of arbitrariness as important representations of the nature of God, and she asserts that the patriarchal position commonly adopted is not attentive to these instances. Awareness of the randomness in Job comes out of an alternative, a feminist way of reading. Thus, Bechtel sees a duality at work in the narrative, a feminist point of view counteracting, or at the very least critiquing, the patriarchal position.

That perspective certainly opens alternatives to readings that conventional views resist, but it does so by merely extending the linearity of the interpretive engagement. An even more satisfying approach, one that builds on the suggestions of alternatives found in feminist readings, removes those boundaries completely. It acknowledges the multiple perspectives that coexist throughout the Book of Job and does not seek to meliorate their differences into a privileged reading of the account. The structure of Job's narrative affirms that each point of view expressed in the story has a subjective validity preserved by its self-containment. Characters do not evolve over the course of the book. Rather, each reaffirms a highly individualized worldview that, for all the action of the narrative, remains unchallenged at the book's conclusion. In consequence, a nonlinear approach stands as the only way to encompass the range of the narrative. This means that a full reading of Job emerges only after recognizing that the structure of the book itself rejects a pattern of linear thinking.

A brief review of the narrative of Job readily illustrates this point. The issue outlined in the first two chapters—whether Job will curse God—acts as a crucial feature in initiating the action, but quickly recedes into the background once Job's sufferings begin. Instead, the emphasis turns from Job's reaction to his afflictions per se to his quest for an understanding of their source. Job and his comforters engage in a seemingly circular debate over the cause of his troubles, with Job protesting innocence and those around him urging him to acknowledge whatever sin on his part provoked the calamities that he has had to endure. No evidence appears on either side of the argument to produce resolution. Reiteration of contrasting views punctuates the discourse and reaffirms everyone's initial positions.

This structural disjunction between God's and Job's construction of events proves inherently frustrating to linear readings, and throughout the narrative it remains a condition that cannot be alleviated by resorting to antithetical conclusions. In the absence of an apparent cause for the suffering, the reader feels the inclination to see this trauma, and by extension life within the narrative, as meaningless. Existentialists believe that a lack of cause logically can lead to only a single conclusion regarding what the effect manifests. For thoughtful critics, however, that still seems reductive. The opening chapters affirm that God clearly behaves in a premeditated if unpredictable fashion. Thus, the intervention of God in the chapters framing the main narrative in fact asserts that randomness does not dominate the action, yet that observation too provides more ambiguity than clarity.

In the end, the Lord rewards Job for showing abject humility and retracting all that he has said. This forwards the message articulated throughout by the three comforters and Elihu: never question the Lord. At the same time, God rebukes the three comforters for speaking untruthfully about Him in saying that the Lord punishes the wicked. The message there seems to be: do not presume to know the reason for God's actions. While the text clearly does not say that those actions are meaningless, it does underscore the daunting task of successfully comprehending them.

Where does that leave readers engaging a work whose central theme seems to be the need to discern structural connections but whose narrative relentlessly obscures the relationship between causes and effects? It results in something like the difficulty articulated by Heisenberg's Uncertainty Principle: perceiving one thing makes something else appear unclear. Engagement with Job's suffering illustrates this quite nicely. Despite the contest agreed upon by God and Satan in chapters 1–2, the fact remains for Job, as he articulates in the final chapter (42:1–6), that he can know his condition, but not the cause of it. For readers, the same perplexity obtains, if at a single remove. We can know the first cause—the Lord as manifest in chapters 1–2 and 38–42—yet remain unable to predict behavior based upon that knowledge. The persistent question that remains is how to find interpretive unity in the Book of Job.

Several factors stand out as coalescing elements or points of cohesion within the narrative. Elements of the discourse adhere to these features, yet this cohesion does not result in sufficient overall unity to resolve the questions, arising from the application of linear interpretive approaches, of the relationships between various aspects of the narrative. The narrative quickly subdivides the issue of suffering into specific issues of how it relates to the will of God (particularly in light of the apparent contest between God and Satan), how an interpretation can or cannot tie materialism to suffering, and how suffering enhances or undercuts one's relationship with God.

The Book of Job does not accommodate the closure of a Cartesian worldview, for closure comes about not simply through an ending but through a full appreciation of the actions that produced that conclusion. Readers never reach that sense of a pattern behind the arbitrary forces governing events in the account. Job's comfortable death at the end of the book offers no more satisfying explanation of his life's purpose than his death by suffering would have.

To begin with, we need to acknowledge that the pleasure of reading Job as a literary rather than a theological document does not lie in its resolution of human difficulties. Rather, it produces imaginative satisfaction through its simultaneous representation of the contradictory aspects of human experience. This results in a narrative that acts both to explain and to obscure our conception of the world that we inhabit. The narrative of the Book of Job asserts that our world cannot be meaningless or random because from the start God oversees the way events in it unfold. At the same time, it shows that we cannot comprehend the world's order, at least strictly in the Newtonian sense, because patterns of cause-and-effect logic do not emerge through analysis.

An alternative response to Cartesian reasoning resists the temptation to characterize the Book of Job as full of contradictions that we need to resolve or ignore. Instead, it approaches the narrative as replete with multiple manifestations capturing the inherent inconsistencies that define our lives. Like the wave/particle theory of light, elements in Job's world thrive within a both/and system of behavior. Rather than confirming the incomprehensibility of our condition, this representation suggests a different approach both to knowing and to expectations of knowledge. (From a theological perspective, of course, this apparent ambivalence enhances rather than impedes one's journey of faith, for it provides the opportunity for the individual to exercise trust in God's divine plan.)

In striving for a sense of coherence in the narrative, we find greater satisfaction in determining the function of the forces that provide internal unity, the elements that affirm the diverse consistencies within the work. By the end of the account of Job' travails, we find no point of view changed and, indeed, every perspective validated because of these varied harmonies. In this way, our readings become richer for understanding how they function.

Certain thematic features display the sort of internal steadfastness that, while not conforming to the interrelatedness of a Cartesian worldview, does function to provide readers with an imaginative stability. Despite the detailed examinations that run through the Book of Job, suffering remains an inexplicable fixture in human experience. The assertions of the comforters and of Elihu in fact give no clearer sense of how or why it occurs. The rebuttals of Job give no clearer sense of its function. And God disdains even to address the topic. Rather than offer any form of consolation regarding the pain experienced in human life, the Book of Job simply affirms its inevitability. A narrow interpretation sees this as a frustration of the investigative process. From a broader perspective, a reader more profitably comprehends it by noting the accuracy of the representation.

Suffering does not yield to rationality. Reading the Book of Job to understand suffering is like reading *King Lear* to learn how to raise children. The power of the narrative comes from its evocation of the agony and confusion familiar to us all when we endure pain for which we can see no logical cause. Efforts to explain the forces that produce such feelings miss the point. The Book of Job reminds us of aspects of our humanity through its forceful representation of its title character.

Not all thematic concerns in the Book of Job, however, evoke familiar impressions. In fact, other issues highlight concepts that seem to have no resonance for us. For instance, with an overt emphasis that modern readers will find disconcerting, throughout the work the narrative advances the view that material prosperity stands as an accurate measure of spiritual growth. Elihu and the comforters of Job never waver in such belief. Job himself does not deny the link between materialism and goodness. Rather, he complains about God's inconsistency when good men do not experience material fortune. And certainly the final condition, the restoration of Job's wealth, gives the lie to anyone who would wish to doubt that relation.

Contemporary readers miss the point if they attempt to reconcile these attitudes with a current reluctance to celebrate material success as an indication of spiritual worth. The point quite simply is not that we do not make such a connection but rather that the individuals in Job did. We need to comprehend and to accept this position before coming to grips with the rest of the narrative. Like those confronted with suffering, readers need not, and perhaps even should not, comprehend the cause behind such an effect. We must, however, recognize materialism as a crucial marker in the way that Job's characters understood their world.

Most disturbingly, at least from the Cartesian perspective, the Book of Job presents God's will as unfathomable at best. Although readers see it as arbitrary and insensitive, for the characters in the narration it remains a powerful mystery. How do we characterize the role that God plays as a force that defines the events of the Book of Job? For us to say simply that Job reinforces the concept that God works in mysterious ways is to ignore what the first two chapters tell us of His motivations. The ambiguity that readers face creates at best a puzzling and at worst a deeply disturbing condition. No matter how we read the role of God in the Book of Job, however, it does not yield to quick, easy, or single-minded explanation.

We can (in a response that does not rely upon presuming the validity of either theism or atheism) acknowledge the fundamental distinction between the Judeo-Christian God and humanity. The two entities operate in different systems, or at least humanity finds itself in a circumscribed system within God's larger system.

What results is a dual sense of alienation and of enclosure. As with the other themes, the point is not to come to a causal explanation of the two systems. Rather, it is to see the enormity of the differences even while coming to a sense of the aspects that define their coexistence. Job strives to portray the ineffable, not to explain it. Though some literary critics may feel unease with the selection of God as the topic of this endeavor, in fact the exercise differs in no way from the commonplace efforts of other writers to represent aesthetics.

Further proof of the inutility of conventional cause-and-effect thinking when applied to the Book of Job comes from the characters themselves, who do not experience the evolutionary changes that linear readings suggest as necessary by-products of traumatic experiences. The narrative introduces Job as a man settled in his ways, "the upright man" who is comfortable practicing orthodox pieties. Events in the narrative suggest that Job behaves as a man habituated to live in a certain way with no real understanding of why he acts as he does.

Over the course of his travails, Job curses the day that he was born. He rejects the view that his sins or the sins of his forebears brought on his sufferings. He asserts that too often in life the wicked prosper and openly wonders why this is so. He wonders why God would punish him with suffering and why God would allow so much wickedness to occur in the world. He goes on to complain to God that God ignores Job's pleas for solace even though God knows that Job is an innocent man.

After God's address, and in the face of undeniable and insuperable power, Job publicly admits that he is an ignorant man who has spoken on matters he does not understand. He then retracts all that he has said. While this may seem a reversal, in fact it affirms the central contention of Job's lamentations. Throughout the book Job asserted that he did not understand why good people suffer. His retraction simply restates that lack of comprehension.

Indeed, while the final lines of the account describe the restoration of Job's material comfort, the narrative remains silent on Job's attitude toward all that has passed. Thus, readers have no indication of any change in perspective beyond Job's last words—the prudent acknowledgment, in the face of the implicit threat of further violence, of an ignorance of God's will. The terseness of his reply hardly suggests an attitude different from that expressed throughout his lamentations. Indeed, when God rebukes Job's comforters, He contrasts their statements with the truths spoken by Job. Thus, although Job may have learned circumspection in the expression of belief, there is no indication of a genuine change from the perspective that he held at the beginning of the narrative.

Likewise, the comforters of Job, despite all that they endure, show no shift in the views that they propounded throughout the book. Indeed, events do nothing if not confirm the validity of their perspectives. Throughout the narrative they have condemned Job as a sinner, brushing aside his protestations of innocence and ignorance. For them, Job's suffering was sufficient proof of guilt. At the end of the book, when God humiliates them for not speaking truthfully as Job had, He in effect confirms their views. Ignorance of guilt is neither an excuse for nor a protection from the sufferings that improper behavior brings on. Thus, as they abase themselves before Job, the man whose sufferings had for them proclaimed his guilt, they embrace the same scenario.

Elihu, the enigmatic figure who bursts on the scene to rebuke Job's comforters for not persisting in their condemnations, also ends the book with his convictions intact. Though younger than any of the others, Elihu has presumed to speak because of a sense of the rightness of his perceptions. Although he says little that differs from the words of the comforters, he completely escapes the humiliations visited upon them. Since nothing appears in the narrative to suggest any alteration in his views, we can assume that the book ends with his perspective also intact.

Finally, although Job's wife and children, as minor characters, may hardly seem worth attention, they too attest to the narrative's resistance to a reconciliation promulgated by traditional readings. Job's children perish as innocent parties, caught up in God's contest with Satan. Job's wife appears briefly, urging Job to "[c]urse God and die." Nothing in the subsequent narration challenges either the arbitrary nature of life experienced by Job's children or the solution to escaping those vicissitudes offered by Job's wife. Their views can be reconciled neither to a benevolent reading nor to an arbitrary view. Rather, they emphasize the singularity of the way each individual perceives the world of this narrative.

With his minion Satan, God emerges as the most enigmatic and least affected character in the book. From the opening, with the peculiar test that He agrees to impose upon Job, to the digressive and defensive catalogue of achievements appearing at the end of the book, God's unsettled and inscrutable nature works at cross-purposes to everything else in the narrative. The seeming insecurity that provokes Him to agree to have His faithful servant tested shows no sign of abatement at the end, when Job has, according to the original terms, successfully endured His trials. Instead, like a schoolyard braggart, God embarks upon an extended description of His achievements and then practices a bit of gratuitous cruelty in His abuse of the comforters. Evidence within the text gives no indication that God has learned anything from all that has occurred, but of course that is the point: were there anything for God to learn, were it possible for God to take instruction, then God would not be God. The imperviousness to events stands as the most powerful reminder that the text can offer of the resoluteness of God's nature.

All this underscores why a linear, exclusionary approach to the Book of Job cannot do justice to its text. For nontheologians or nonphilosophers, reconciling the narrative's paradoxes by bringing its sequence of events together to form one lesson or another—God's will is mysterious yet nonetheless provident, or life is arbitrary and attempting to impose meaning upon it misses the point. The stories encompassed by the Book of Job have a profound impact because, through the integrity of individual perspectives, they steadfastly resist closure.

The Book of Job offers no definitive explanation of life, either hopeful or despairing. It provides no prescription for understanding our world or Job's. Rather, it very skillfully captures the individuality that characterizes the way that we each—readers and characters—live. Job's narrative celebrates life's multiplicities and its arbitrariness.

The principles of chaos theory free readers of Job from the imperative to resolve linear contradictions. The unity of the narrative resides in the amalgamation of experiences that it chronicles. These experiences do not form a seamless whole. Rather, they articulate disruptive and contradictory perceptions that cannot be resolved because of the independence of individual consciousnesses.

Nonlinear thinking enables the literary critics at least to take God on His own terms, as unknowable, rather than to press for Newtonian closure to explain His actions. At the same time, this approach resists the pious inclination to accept God's will without question. Indeed, every character in the narration has articulated his or her explanation of the universe, and the narrative has rewarded each by validating each explanation. While linear views seek to make the narrative fit a single pattern, nonlinear thinking makes acceptable the irresolvable nature of Job's world.

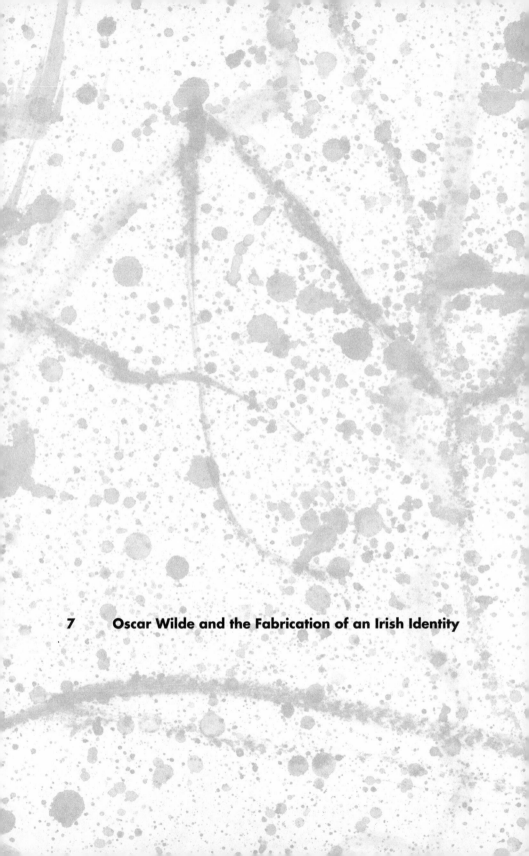

7   Oscar Wilde and the Fabrication of an Irish Identity

—But do you know what a nation means? says John Wyse.
—Yes, says Bloom.
—What is it? says John Wyse.
—A nation? says Bloom. A nation is the same people living in the same place.
—By God, then, says Ned, laughing, if that's so I'm a nation for I'm living in the same place for the past five years.

So of course everyone had the laugh at Bloom and says he, trying to muck out of it:
—Or also living in different places.
—That covers my case, says Joe.
—What is your nation if I may ask? says the citizen.
—Ireland, says Bloom. I was born here. Ireland.
JAMES JOYCE, ULYSSES, 12.1419–31

ANY U.S. CITIZEN who has traveled for any length of time in Europe has had the experience of enduring at least once, and usually with greater frequency, unsolicited civics, history, diplomatic, or cultural lessons that always begin in the same fashion: "You Americans. . . ." Customs agents, cabdrivers, hotel concierges, waiters, and a vast array of other sundry acquaintances all feel qualified to tell us what is wrong with our country, our national character, and our general demeanor, because each feels confident that he or she knows exactly not only what an American is but what an American should be. The frustration that comes from enduring one of these lectures stems at least in part from an acute awareness of the complex features that make up the nature of any individual American and from a sure sense of the heterogeneity that characterizes the United States.

Despite the optimistic view held by our nation's forebears of our ability to coalesce—summed up in the motto "e pluribus unum"—the diverse elements of the American identity do not readily blend into a seamless whole. Indeed, heterogeneity stands as the element that best captures our national character. From this perspective, it seems a reasonable extrapolation to admit a measure of multiplicity inherent in any society, and thus remaining attentive to the contradictory features of the American psyche may facilitate comprehension of the subjective representations of national identity in the works of authors from any country. The methods for discerning meaning advanced in this study may serve as a means for negotiating that subjectivity.

In readings that pay attention to nationality as part of the interpretive process, the usefulness of an approach that accommodates narrative contradiction and multiplicity quickly becomes apparent. The epigraph from Ulysses quoted above illustrates the difficulties that quickly accrue in attempting to pinpoint the features of a national identity, in this case Irishness. While humorously underscoring the slipperiness of language, the exchange in Barney Kiernan's pub more precisely highlights an all-too-human tendency to mistake a personal concept for a generally accepted condition and to frame observations from that misprision. Bloom's ineffectual response to shifting interpretations of the term comes from his attempt to accommodate all possible contingencies by creating a sprawling definition of nationhood. Because he persists in applying an either/or system of thought that cannot sustain the multiplicities of his topic, he succeeds only in looking foolish.

Bloom's experiences have recently taken on a new pertinence, with the literature of cultural identity becoming an increasingly important topic for many contemporary critics. Given the difficulties that arise from applying conventional methods to examinations of national character, it seems appropriate for this study to use that subgenre as a final example of the efficacy of nonlinear interpretive methods. With postcolonial studies offering lively debates over the fundamental sense of terms like *race* and *ethnicity*, numerous readers are feeling a growing unease over how to integrate an understanding of cultural context into a literary interpretation.[1]

Of course, ethnic studies can be pursued in any number of directions, and a pronounced interest over the last two decades of the twentieth century in the impact of postcolonialism, imperialism, and nationalism has created an abundance of examples upon which to draw.[2] From this interest a number of critics have devoted attention to the impact of postcolonialism. The conflicted nature of this approach has been especially apparent in studies of Irish writers—inhabitants of Europe, the predominant society of early modern colonizers, yet victims of an imperial regime. A great deal of attention has been given to the works of James Joyce, but other figures have also garnered a share of this interest.[3] Whomever we might choose to examine, the salient point is that through concepts of postcolonialism we see a work from heretofore ignored perspectives. At the same time, as with other Cartesian-grounded analyses, prescriptiveness circumscribes the most popular approaches.

Among a number of interesting studies, Declan Kiberd's *Inventing Ireland* remains perhaps the most useful, and certainly the most popular, of the recent books on manifestations of Irish identity in literature. Reflective of the postcolonial temperament, Kiberd constructs his perspective of Irishness with a very vocal awareness of the influence of England, the country's colonizer for nearly a millennium. The assessment that results certainly illustrates Kiberd's skills as a close reader and a social critic, but it also highlights the problems that arise from a linear approach to national identity.

Kiberd employs a straightforward, Cartesian assessment of the impact of nearly 1,000 years of British mores on the Celtic imagination. Kiberd asserts that English occupation has led to the deracination of Irish identity. He goes on to privilege the twentieth century, beginning with the Easter Rising of 1916, as a period for the reinvention of the Irish character. Of interest, especially in terms of this study, is Kiberd's emphasis on the self-creation—through the nation's writers—of Irishness.

While Kiberd dutifully employs reference to both/and modes of perception, he stops well short of embracing subjectivity. Instead, he achieves both a measure of diversity and a reassuring equilibrium by privileging the dualities of self and other. By highlighting the importance of authenticity—in the sense advocated by Lionel Trilling—he foregrounds the validation of self-dramatization by the other. This leads, as Peter Kuch has already noted, to wavering "between a constructivist and an essentialist view of Irish identity."[4] That is to say, he oscillates between an objective and a subjective view. Ultimately, this becomes an effort to secure closure by imposing new limitations on an approach that has distinguished itself by overturning old restrictions. (In this fashion, Kiberd runs up against problems similar to those faced by Derrida and outlined in Mary Poovey's essay "Feminism and Deconstruction.")

Looking back at this chapter's epigraph, the reader can understand Kiberd's dilemma. Removing either aspect of the perspective undermines the sense of complexity and contradiction that animates postcolonial thinking. Denying subjectivity within the Irish nature threatens the very individuality that postcolonial writers seek to recover from the imperial experience. Asserting that an objective Irishness does not exist would mean that the term changes from individual to individual, and so for conventional literary criticism it would have at best highly limited applicability. In a world of subjective readings, however, the term *Irishness* has no greater or lesser specificity than does any other word. What becomes significant is how the individual reads and understands that concept, for one's comprehension of it alone will inform its interpretive impact.

Such a view would impede critical discussions informed by Cartesian logic. This chapter, however, with its recourse to non-Newtonian thinking, offers an alternative method for understanding for Leopold Bloom, Declan Kiberd, and anyone else concerned with the way Irish, and by extension any national, identity is manifest in literature. Like a drop of water moving in a turbulent stream, identity in literature encompasses individual features that remain unpredictable while existing within very clearly defined borders. I am seeking to apply to the issue of ethnicity in literature those methods brought forward in the preceding chapters' analyses of the efficacy of other contemporary methodologies. To begin, I wish to assert the assumptions in this approach to ethnicity in literature that differentiate it from preceding examinations.

As I have throughout this study, I advocate here an inversion of Cartesian logic. I foreground a method privileging flux rather than closure. The title of this chapter plays off that preference for mutability by introducing a term, *fabrication*, that simultaneously evokes concepts of genuine and counterfeit and suggests a plurality similar to that characterizing notions of Irish identity. Joyce uses the same punning approach in the famous lines at the end of *A Portrait of the Artist as a Young Man*, which capture both the uncertainty and the enduring attraction of national identity: "I go to encounter for the millionth time the reality of experience and to forge in the smithy of my soul the uncreated conscience of my race."[5] Stephen Dedalus highlights the incipient, unstable condition of Irish identity, and he articulates my own view that the construction of national character stands open to any individual willing to replicate his gesture.

As Joyce's protagonist suggests, Irish identity comes into being or remains absent as a reader's choice, part of the process of comprehending a work. This means that I can see W. B. Yeats' 1899 collection of poems, *The Wind among the Reeds*, as growing out of a general interest in mysticism or as coming from an Anglo-Irish folk culture. Similarly, I could view James Joyce's *Ulysses* as a novel typifying European angst or just as readily take it as a portrait of Irish-Catholic trauma. Or, as I will explore in this chapter, I could label *The Importance of Being Earnest* an English farce or just as easily call it an Irish satire. Further, no two readers will have exactly the same understanding of the elements that constitute any designation, a condition that has implications for the nature of Irish identity.

At the same time, invoking Irishness in an interpretation of any work—novel, poem, or play—signals what has become a fairly familiar strategy for reading. It acknowledges certain cultural forces shaping the composition of the work, and it suggests that attentiveness to those forces will inform one's interpretations. What remains an open question is how most effectively to apply that feature to an overall conception of what is there on the printed page.

While the reader occupies a central role in the fabrication of meaning, no one attentive to the impact of the composition process upon how we understand literature would advocate ignoring the background of the writer. As many contemporary critics have argued, a writer's cultural heritage inevitably exerts a shaping force upon the art that he or she produces and by extension upon what we try to comprehend. Indeed, if we relied upon the content of a work as the sole criterion for Irishness, then we could make a convincing argument that the novels of J. P. Donleavy and Thomas Flanagan would fall within that category, while the writings of Samuel Beckett and John Banville would not.

Engaging the writer's cultural heritage remains an important part of the interpretive process, but discerning its features becomes as complicated for us as defining a nation is for Bloom. My position when reading someone like Oscar Wilde necessarily embraces interpretive multiplicity. I assume that

Irishness informs his writing, but I also understand that term as fraught with indeterminacy. What I recognize as an Irish identity will come from the sense of the term that I bring to Wilde's work, and it very likely will change with each encounter. Further, the author's own views can have no interest for me. I can read Graham Greene as a Catholic writer, for instance, without feeling that I must discern his notion of Catholicism before proceeding. Indeed, given my views on subjectivity, I inevitably will apply my own conception of Catholicism to my interpretations of his work. Similarly, it is not important, for instance, whether Wilde thought of himself as Irish or as someone writing from an Irish perspective, but my impression of his Irish background has a profound effect upon the way I see his writing.

Thus, I welcome the recognition that characterizing Irishness in literature remains both a contingent and an unstable project. As Heisenberg's Uncertainty Principle dictates, applying the process entails giving primacy to selected elements in a work of literature that characterize what the reader loosely conceives of as Irishness, while shifting attention away from other elements. These factors necessarily vary from individual to individual, and they reflect the impressionistic nature of any effort to discern identity. Irishness always emerges from personal conceptions, and so to understand the Irish aspects of Wilde, I need to understand how I construct it. Grasping its composition in turn helps me comprehend the assumptions that I bring to any reading. This is not an exercise in circularity. Rather, it reflects efforts to delineate the necessary ambiguity inherent in any critical inquiry. (Understanding this disparity becomes crucial when I discuss Wilde's Irishness with another reader, given the inevitable divergence between my concept of identity and his or hers.)

Whether Irishness originates within the nature of the author, emerges from a totalizing view summing up an entire culture, or manifests itself in selected cultural artifacts, the voice identifying this Irishness inevitably originates in a single imagination—that of the person who classifies it. The individual consciousness overturns rather than enforces stability. Despite the common reference point in the body of cultural artifacts that shape one's sense of Irishness, perspectives coming from the minds of diverse readers or critics, and presumably changing to greater or lesser degrees from person to person, cause every project in search of identity to emerge as a subjective endeavor. At the same time, acknowledging subjectivity does not resolve how a particular conception of Irishness informs interpretive options and in effect privileges certain meanings that I derive from the writings of Wilde. More often than not, it merely highlights the ambiguities that come into play.

Consequently, despite the centrality of Irishness to my discussion of *The Importance of Being Earnest,* I will not attempt to define the term. Because

I see Irish identity as residing within the individual consciousness, its distinguishing features will vary greatly from individual to individual. (Certainly, some impressions may overlap, but, as with any highly charged subject, even the overlapping will be subject to highly individualistic interpretations. Imagine a dozen people of any nationality being asked to define the predominant characteristics that distinguish that nationality. Their general answers might very well reflect a commonality. Then, ask each what personal traits define him or her as a member of that national group. The responses would be as varied as the number queried.) The elements that an individual recognizes as characteristic of an Irish nature become evident through the interpretive process, so stepping out of specific readings to offer a broadly applicable version of Irishness would give a false impression of stability. Everyone reads a different Irish identity into a work. This does not mean that the term itself has no application in critical discourse, but understanding its usefulness requires the adoption of a new way of thinking about identity that resists the imposed closure of Cartesian logic.

Post-Einsteinian physics—an interpretive system that freely embraces subjectivity and yet enjoys high credibility as a rigorous method of inquiry—offers effective metaphors for managing the levels of uncertainty inherent in discussions of perceptions of Irish identity. The systematized subjectivity of twentieth-century physics accommodates ambiguity without the lack of an either/or resolution undermining the validity of its conclusions. (Of course, by this I do not mean to imply unanimity among physicists regarding the findings of the Copenhagen group.) Indeed, its intellectual strength rests upon the recognition that multiple and even contradictory points of view can exist simultaneously. I would like to use aspects of post-Einsteinian science to show how similar perspectives can inform views of Irish identity.

As part of the process of interpretation, I have the choice of setting the parameters of an Irish identity, imposing it or not upon various writings, and generating readings based upon my ability to dictate this identity. This function stands as the counterpart of the observer in Schrödinger's thought experiment about the cat, an illustration of the determinism exerted by the observer in quantum physics, elaborated upon in the appendix. Bringing cultural identity into existence in *The Importance of Being Earnest* does not hinge on the recognition of ethnic features or national sympathies inherent in the consciousness of Oscar Wilde or in the language of the play. Nor does it hinge upon whether Wilde's writing demonstrates that he thought of himself as Irish. Nor does the recognition of traits called "Irish" in any reading of the play produce a stable reading. Rather, Irishness comes from and continually evolves within the imagination of the individual who perceives it, and, whenever invoked, fundamentally changes the view of the work to which it is being applied.

In Schrödinger's experiment, the observer who determines the cat's viability does not worry whether the animal in question believes itself alive or dead. Nor in the case of Heisenberg's Uncertainty Principle does the physicist who measures an electron express nostalgia for the makeup of the unobserved particle before measurement changed its speed or direction. Likewise, despite my concern with Irish identity in *The Importance of Being Earnest*, I have no interest in what Wilde believed. (Indeed, turning to Wilde for direction on reading identity in the play constitutes an affinity for methodologies I do not endorse.) Nor do I care about the constitution of the text before I encountered it. Rather, I approach the play seeking ways of forming a unified, though transitory and subjective, aesthetic experience that engages my imagination in a coherent fashion.

This interpretative method does not make my awareness of Irishness in *The Importance of Being Earnest* any less authentic—just as Schrödinger's cat is no less alive for having its continuing vitality confirmed only upon being perceived and Heisenberg's electrons are not less real for changing speed or position whenever they are measured. It does, however, treat Irish identity as a force that disrupts rather than stabilizes interpretative positions about the work of Wilde or anyone else. This sense of the subjectivity of Irish identity can help us all construct texts of *The Importance of Being Earnest*.

Throughout this study, I have asserted my belief in the view that a work of art has no existence save in the mind of a reader. Each act of imagining grows out of concepts slightly or greatly different from those informing previous imaginings. Consequently, when I think of *The Importance of Being Earnest* as a drama informed by an Irish identity, I am configuring its fundamental composition. We already detect this sort of variation in the different descriptions of the play found in received readings. Contemporary critics have opinions of it ranging from a farcical evocation of the mores and manners of late-nineteenth-century England, to a work profoundly shaped by the tradition of British melodrama from which it emerges, to a powerful philosophical inquisition of the conventional values of Victorian literature and society.[6] None of these studies questions the stability of the English milieu as the foundation of the play. Each simply makes a decision about its viability—like that of Schrödinger's cat—without apparently being aware of it. If, on the other hand, someone facing the same choice gives the play an Irish identity, whatever that might be, then a different work or works emerge. The gentle or not so gentle satire on the foibles of the manners, institutions, and ambitions of the English upper-middle-class presumed by the works cited above takes on an alternate form.

The approach taken here challenges the dominant objectification of Irish identity practiced by many readers. Unconsciously mimicking Bloom's sense of nationhood, critics who succumb to generalizations founded upon their own points of view set up readings that employ the term *Irishness* as if it were a universally accepted proposition, yet they do not trouble themselves to articulate clearly what they believe the term to mean. Jerusha Mc-Cormack, for example, has published *Wilde the Irishman,* a collection of essays by various Irish critics who offer their opinions on a variety of topics related to Wilde's Irishness. Despite some fine pieces, such as Deirdre Toomey's comparison of elements of Wilde's creative process with generalizations about Irishness, assumptions that underlie the volume's structure cloud rather than clarify the issue. McCormack as editor never defines what she means by *Irishness,* especially as it relates to Wilde. This choice would certainly be acceptable if its inherent subjectivity were acknowledged. However, although various essayists offer wide-ranging comments on aspects of Wilde's Irish identity, the volume makes no effort either to reconcile or to distinguish between diverse views. Instead, McCormack leaves the reader with the impression that she believes that all her contributors are talking about the same thing, an essential Irishness that everyone understands and so never needs defining.

Critics have already noted that reading *The Importance of Being Earnest* as an Irish play allows the marginalized figures of Jack Worthing and Algernon Moncrieff to appear as manifestations of the alienation that shaped the creative process of Wilde the Irishman writing for English audiences. Declan Kiberd has nicely extended that line of thought to suggest that nearly all of the characters in *The Importance of Being Earnest* occupy a position on the periphery of English society, reflecting Wilde's sense of where he had been relegated because of his Irish nature. In my approach, seeing Irishness in the play goes well beyond reconfiguring familiar characterizations or re-positioning traditional roles to accommodate nationalist sentiments. An Irish point of view alters perceptions of diverse issues—ethics, sensuality, and class—that mark the play's parameters, and in doing so it reconfigures the elemental features of the text.

Of course, merely using the terms *English* and *Irish* in a reading of *The Importance of Being Earnest* may seem to reimpose the essentialist views that I have already argued against. However, my assumption of the inherent subjectivity of the process prevents this, for my sense of Englishness or Irishness reconfigures the play in a fashion different from anyone else's. To this end, the integrity of the image of the gentle comedy cherished by the critics cited above crumbles when I choose to make Irish identity a condition central to the formation of my readings, and I replace that view with a reading no less transitory. Foregrounding the Irish cultural context from which the creative process of Oscar Wilde emerged rebuffs inclinations to label the work as a tolerant lampoon of British foibles and instead invites an emphasis on alternative features.

Consequently, Irishness becomes the starting point for any number of different constructions of the play. The following examples do not offer a reading to counter those of the critics already cited. Rather, they present a series of alternative manifestations of the play, each brought into being by a different concept of Irish identity and each part of its complete comprehension.

When I think about elective affinities within *The Importance of Being Earnest*, the radical differences imposed by identity become clear. Many critics, for example, labeling the play as British in nature, invite the characterization of Cecily Cardew and Gwendolen Fairfax as ingénues typical of nineteenth-century melodrama, chafing against whimsical strictures imposed upon them by English society. A fairly typical piece of dialogue midway through the play may at first seem to enforce that view:

GWENDOLEN. Mr Worthing, I have something very particular to ask you. Much depends upon your reply.

CECILY. Gwendolen, our common sense is invaluable. Mr Moncrieff, kindly answer me the following questions. Why did you pretend to be my guardian's brother?

ALGERNON. In order that I might have the opportunity of meeting you.

CECILY. [*To Gwendolen.*] That certainly seems a satisfactory explanation, does it not?

GWENDOLEN. Yes, dear, if you can believe him.

CECILY. I don't. But that does not affect the wonderful beauty of his answer.

GWENDOLEN. True. In matters of grave importance, style, not sincerity is the vital thing. Mr Worthing, what explanation can you offer me for pretending to have a brother? Was it in order that you might have an opportunity of coming up to town to see me as often as possible?

JACK. Can you doubt it, Miss Fairfax?

GWENDOLEN. I have the gravest doubts upon the subject. But I intend to crush them. This is not the moment for German scepticism.[7]

In fact, a persistent relativism charges these lines with a direct appeal to the reader's subjectivity. While the wit of this exchange remains constant, its humor varies inversely to its national affiliation. In the received interpretations that characterize the scene as informed by an English consciousness, Gwendolen and Cecily reflect the attitudes of women who have learned to manipulate the institutions of the dominant culture, playing upon conventions to direct the conduct of Jack and Algy, and then setting aside those conditions as it suits them. Their complete integration into society makes their manipulation of its forms charming.

However, seeing the play from an Irish point of view, in this case one that pays special attention to the politics of hegemony, makes it difficult to accept the apparent inconsistencies in the natures of the two women as little more than innocuous flightiness. Instead, a number of alternative, subversive implications present themselves: I may view Gwendolen and Cecily as typifying the hypocrisy of English society; or I can find, in their reversal of conventional gender roles, a reflection of how British institutions actually function; or I might discern them offering a blueprint to outsiders seeking models for resisting the colonizing mentality of a dominant group. In any case, Heisenberg's Uncertainty Principle applies, for through my act of reading—that is, the recognition of key elements of individuals' personalities—I have changed the structure of their roles in the play.

Identity derived from national character has an impact on the way that a reader constructs even minor figures like Miss Prism and the Reverend Chasuble. When that identity takes on a subjective character, it challenges any presumption of interpretive stability. Contextualizing the following exchange on sexual appetites, for example, will ineluctably shape what I see as the nature of these individuals:

> CHASUBLE. Were I fortunate enough to be Miss Prism's pupil, I would hang upon her lips. [*Miss Prism glares.*] I spoke metaphorically—My metaphor was drawn from bees.
>
>   *   *   *
>
> MISS PRISM. [*Sententiously.*] And you do not seem to realize, dear Doctor, that by persistently remaining single, a man converts himself into a permanent public temptation. Men should be more careful; this very celibacy leads weaker vessels astray.
>
> CHASUBLE. But is a man not equally attractive when married?
>
> MISS PRISM. No married man is ever attractive except to his wife.
>
> CHASUBLE. And often, I've been told, not even to her.
>
> MISS PRISM. That depends on the intellectual sympathies of the woman. Maturity can always be depended upon. Ripeness can be trusted. Young women are green. [*Dr. Chasuble starts.*] I spoke horticulturally. My metaphor was drawn from fruits. (502, 505)

Viewing these conversations as expressions of sentiments by characters of the dominant culture secure in their positions in society may dispose me to put them in a benevolent context, making their repressed sexuality a winsome trait. The shy innocence of their awkward articulations gives the exchange an engaging and harmless allure.

If, however, my reading instead recognizes an Irish point of view, synonymous with the role of the outsider deprived of the right of ordinary expression, as contextualizing the sexuality of these individuals, then enchantment disappears. Instead, the scene turns on their vulnerability, and it leads me to consider the power of their appetites and the perverse effects of repression, rather than the quaintness of their embarrassment. This in turn emphasizes the corrosive influence of dominant English culture as it inhibits the open articulation of normal human feelings. In consequence, equivocation, no matter how banal or transparent, seems the only way to proceed in such a society. Individuals in the play take on multiple roles because to survive they must acquire the ability to blend into English society.

Indeed, once I acknowledge the possibility of constructing any number of different plays by being attentive to Irish associations, then subversion rather than melioration comes to dominate the work I am interpreting, reflected even in the seemingly quintessentially benign English character Lane, Algernon's butler:

> ALGERNON. Lane, I see from your book that on Thursday night, when Lord Shoreham and Mr Worthing were dining with me, eight bottles of champagne are entered as having been consumed.
>
> LANE. Yes, sir; eight bottles and a pint.
>
> ALGERNON. Why is it that at a bachelor's establishment the servants invariably drink the champagne? I ask merely for information.
>
> LANE. I attribute it to the superior quality of the wine, sir. I have often observed that in married households the champagne is rarely of a first-rate brand.
>
> ALGERNON. Good Heavens! Is marriage so demoralizing as that?
>
> LANE. I believe it *is* [Wilde's emphasis] a very pleasant state, sir. I have had very little experience of it myself up to the present. I have only been married once. That was in consequence of a misunderstanding between myself and a young person.
>
> ALGERNON. [*Languidly.*] I don't know that I am much interested in your family life, Lane.
>
> LANE. No sir; it is not a very interesting subject. I never think of it myself. (480–81)

Anglophilic P. G. Wodehouse enthusiasts may be quick to see Lane as merely a charming avatar of Jeeves. That sentimental English context leads to the assumption that Lane's tact protects Algernon from having to admit to drinking too much champagne.

When I consider the characters as operating out of an Irish identity defined by power relationships, I become attentive to the implications of Lane's dismissive gesture of marriage and of the "young person" who had been his wife. His motives or acts hardly seem benevolent, for Lane's callousness replicates the harshest aspects of the power relationship already established between himself and Algernon, while excluding all of its meliorating features. Indeed, his behavior reflects just the sort of exploitive, colonizing impulse that critics like Kiberd see operating at a microcosmic level in consequence of the macrocosmic influence of imperialism. By emphasizing a vulnerability that comes out of one sense of the Irishness of the play, I become attentive to the social ramifications of Lane's attitude toward marriage. His brutal dismissal of his married life — "I never think of it myself" — evokes images of abandonment, poverty, and degradation. That in turn changes the status of the marriage plot that informs the central action of Wilde's drama from lighthearted burlesque to bitter satire.

In the most damning construction of national identity in the play, characters stand as self-indicted, mock-Irish figures whose desire to ape the English has only corrupted them. This is particularly evident in Lady Bracknell. From the perspective of the Irish as a marginalized group sensitive to the exclusionary inclinations of English society, it is easy to recognize Lady Bracknell as a nouveau riche parvenue of the worst sort, very much outside the class with which she attempts to associate herself.[8] Her position in society becomes eminently clear in the exchange that she has with Jack when he seeks permission to marry Gwendolen. Lady Bracknell's outline of the desirable characteristics of a prospective son-in-law sketches a view of the world as far outside the mainstream as that of the most eccentric of Wilde's creations:

> Mr Worthing, I confess that I feel somewhat bewildered by what you have just told me. To be born, or at any rate bred, in a hand-bag, whether it had handles or not, seems to me to display a contempt for the ordinary decencies of family life that reminds one of the worst excesses of the French Revolution. And I presume you know what that unfortunate movement led to? As for the particular locality in which the hand-bag was found, a cloak-room at a railway station might serve to conceal a social indiscretion — has probably, indeed been used for that purpose before now — but it could hardly be regarded as an assured basis for a recognized position in good society.
>
>   *   *   *
>
> You can hardly imagine that I and Lord Bracknell would dream of allowing our only daughter — a girl brought up with the utmost care — to marry into a cloak-room and form an alliance with a parcel. Good morning, Mr Worthing. (495)

In language no less blunt than the contemptuous dismissal of the English by Joyce's Prof. McHugh — "I speak the tongue of a race the acme of whose mentality is the maxim: time is money" (U, 7.555–56) — Lady Bracknell unconsciously indicts herself as guilty of the same provincial mendacity.

Joyce's summation of the English mentality enforces the usefulness of structuring the scene from a particular Irish perspective. In the Aeolus chapter of *Ulysses*, where McHugh's comments appear, the discourse has focused attention on the debased mercantilism of the English through frequent invocations of the Irish-Greek/English-Roman analogue. Just as the English language has usurped Prof. McHugh's access to Irish, the English mentality endeavors to circumscribe his nation's imaginative freedom. In *The Impor-

tance of Being Earnest a similar association has emerged that goes beyond the quaint snobbery of an English view of Lady Bracknell. Instead it offers a glimpse of the soul-deadening influence of the materialist world of the colonizers, one that unfailingly pollutes the culture that it has come to dominate. In this light, Lady Bracknell and her values represent more than simply the usurpation of Jack's life as a bachelor. They stand ready to corrupt his very humanity.

The final lines of *The Importance of Being Earnest* aptly illustrate how different plays emerge from my decision to read an Irish identity into it:

JACK. Gwendolen, it is a terrible thing for a man to find out suddenly that all his life he has been speaking nothing but the truth. Can you forgive me?
GWENDOLEN. I can. For I feel that you are sure to change.

*   *   *

LADY BRACKNELL. My nephew, you seem to be displaying signs of triviality.
JACK. On the contrary, Aunt Augusta, I've now realized for the first time in my life the vital Importance of Being Earnest. (537–38)

Once again, critics, like those cited above, who have contextualized the play within the secure attitudes of an English perspective have removed all menace from this conclusion. The contradictions in Jack's behavior underscore his nonchalance, and Lady Bracknell's criticism merely echoes the play's subtitle: *A Trivial Comedy for Serious People*. The double entendre of *Earnest* and *Ernest* in the last line allows Jack to give an answer that will satisfy the contradictory needs of Lady Bracknell and of Gwendolen. It thus calls to mind the wit at the center of *The Importance of Being Earnest* and gives the pleasure of hearing the play end upon a pun that extends its harmless ambiguity.

When I adopt an Irish point of view that emphasizes the significance of using language to avoid closure, however, the homophonic mutability of Jack's response must lead to a far harsher reading. Jack's reply in fact subverts what it ostensibly establishes. He attests to the impotence of being earnest by using wordplay to drain his remarks of all sincerity. With this dexterous articulation, Jack shows that he has overcome the repercussions of the uncomfortable revelation "that all his life he has been speaking nothing but the truth" by becoming adept at manipulating the way others comprehend a situation. Now, he no longer finds himself constrained to adopt one pose in the country and another in the city. Rather, he has learned how language allows him to sustain both simultaneously. This makes *The Importance of Being Earnest* for me the very embodiment of its subtitle—a trivial play for serious (though not principled) people—for it has shown how even the most apparently flippant rhetorical stance can produce highly effective control.

While the directness of being earnest robs Jack's language of its power, the ambiguity of being earnest/Ernest gives him mastery of the situation.

The very slipperiness of language, highlighted in the opening pages of this study and reiterated in these examples, serves to sustain the approach that I am advocating. I have claimed that every interpretive effort changes the text under examination so that every reading is literally of a different work. The concepts of Schrödinger's Cat and Heisenberg's Uncertainty Principle are crucial to this claim. They demonstrate the volatility of any act of observation and exemplify how no two readings ever talk about the same piece of writing. Any effort to give meaning to *The Importance of Being Earnest* always refers to a play that exists only in a single, highly subjective experience.

At the same time, calling a reading subjective is not the same as saying it is irrelevant. Indeed, subjectivity stands as an important concept for understanding the evolving reading process that an aesthetically satisfying work like *The Importance of Being Earnest* will stimulate. One critic publishes subjective views for the same reason that another publishes putatively objective ones: not because any reach a definitive interpretation, but rather because watching the interpretive process unfold remains valuable not only to the critic who instigates it but to any interested reader who observes it.

As I noted at the beginning of this chapter, a nationalist disposition within individual readings of *The Importance of Being Earnest* radically reforms the work under consideration yet does so from an overtly personalized point of view. Indeed, the Irish character remains an unstable, changeable condition that calls into question its efficacy as a secure measure of any aspect of writing. The subjectivity of the concept makes it useless for critics to presume to exchange ideas about a fixed Irish identity or to imagine the possibility of regularizing its impact upon any work that they all have read. Rather, an individual interacts with literature to produce a text unique to each engagement, and interpretations stand out as a form of creation, self-contained and transient. In short, our critical writings do not explain any piece of literature, but rather dramatize our creation of it. In consequence, the best of these demonstrations provoke readers to make further explorations of their own responses, while the worst remain self-centered performances.

If a person is able to accept the paradigm of post-Einsteinian thought, exemplified by the story of Schrödinger's cat and the tenets of Heisenberg's Uncertainty Principle, the aims and values of literary criticism change radically. With these concepts as a guide, certitude and closure no longer dominate our interpretive impulses. Instead, it becomes possible to exchange with other readers aesthetic impressions based upon common interests, such as the impact of nationality, without falling into a reductive articulation of a concept such as Irish identity.

8   **What Is to Be Done?**

THE DIVERSE EXAMPLES of the previous chapters show how a reader can apply nonlinear analysis to literary studies. Nonetheless, I cannot help feeling that the question of where a reader can take this methodology remains a prominent issue. Allow me then to review the suggestions that I have made as a way of summarizing my argument.

Cause-and-effect thinking exerts a powerful hold upon the way that we all perceive our surroundings. Indeed, careful readers have doubtless already noted that, in the midst of all that I have written about the inhibiting influence of Cartesian logic, unmistakable signs of the authority of that form of thinking recur throughout my argument. The difficulty of overcoming the habituation of conventional modes of analysis does not manifest itself uniquely in my work. In fact, none of the writers whom I cite for their ability to apply the concepts of nonlinear thinking to literary studies has been able to overcome completely the pressure to formulate hypotheses based upon cause-and-effect associations. This is an environment where both readers and writers find linear assumptions constantly impinging upon their perceptions of the world. It raises the question of how the concepts of chaos and complexity theories can produce interpretations that match the diversity of the reading experience.

I think that the effort to inculcate nonlinear thinking into literary analysis begins with a change in the expectations that we bring to the process. As currently structured, academic criticism strives toward resolution and seeks to abolish ambiguity. These gestures run counter to the impressions that we ordinarily derive in our individual engagement with a text, and, consequently, no matter how clever they seem, they remain inadequate to our needs. Admitting the complexity of the reading process and recognizing the failure of conventional interpretations to facilitate that experience will go a long way toward reorienting interpretive assumptions. If we can accept the necessity of making public commentary as inclusive as private apprehension, then the institutionalized interpretive process will have undergone the paradigmatic shift in goals necessary to reconfigure its operative analytic system.

Obviously, the reformation of standards of assessment stands as an enormous transformation, and the success of such a project is much more likely to come from a willingness to institute incremental adjustments than from efforts to implement sweeping changes. The first step in such alterations quite simply is an incorporation into operative interpretations the disposition advocated in criticism for centuries but never successfully adopted: a cultivation of ambiguity. Given the failures of the past, this may seem a quixotic endeavor. The difference between earlier efforts and the proposals that I am making in this study, however, lies in the expressive means now available to critics. Thanks to the hard sciences, we now have the ability to articulate our views in a pluralistic fashion that has a credibility heretofore lacking.

In a closed Cartesian world the tasks of sustaining multiple perspectives and forestalling closure for as long as possible have proved to be impossible to carry out. Derrida and others might speak enthusiastically of "endless deferral," but they form these descriptions from the linear lexicon of closure. As I noted in the first chapter, Reed Way Dasenbrock has examined specifically how Derrida's efforts to sustain pluralities have succumbed to the demands of Cartesian criticism (though this latter term is my designation and not Dasenbrock's), because Derrida's discourse remains imbedded within those conventions.[1] The polarities in which Deconstructionists' arguments exist can never step outside a world defined by assumptions antipathetic to their ends. This resulting paralysis is inevitable given the constrictions imposed upon their discourse. As long as critical theorists advocate the pursuit of ambiguity by using a metaphoric system that constitutes itself through images of resolution, their efforts are bound to be frustrated. The New Physics now offers ways around that obstacle.

The most important step toward change involves language. As illustrated by the example of Schrödinger's Cat (a thought experiment detailed in the appendix), when someone accepts a different system for describing his or her surroundings, the world itself changes. Concepts that heretofore seemed impossible to accept become eminently plausible. Indeed, critics such as Hayles, Hawkins, Kuberski, and Demastes have already shown how it is possible to apply that system of discourse to post-Modern literature. Now it becomes a matter of determination to push that application further and use this new lexicon to illuminate our readings of more-traditional literature.

Once the language of criticism changes, larger conditions will become amenable to modification. Instead of pointing all one's efforts toward the validation of an isolated conclusion, interpretations can elucidate the process itself. That will entail eschewing the celebration of insights derived from a single point of view and instead concentrating on highlighting options for multiple responses within a work. Showing readers where a discourse raises ambiguities to which we each respond in an independent manner will give them a great deal more satisfaction than efforts to foreground some critic's ingenuity in the construction of a prescriptive interpretation. Further, that reorientation enables the recognition of multiplicity not just in selected avant-garde writing but in every piece of literature that a reader takes up. Because we can now speak in a less inhibited way about how we perceive literature, we can come to understand that all along we have been perceiving it in a fashion far more complex than we have had the ability to acknowledge.

Ultimately, we will implement nonlinear analysis when we embrace the complicated integrity of the works we examine. Scientists make their greatest discoveries of anomalous behavior in entities that they study when they take as a given the overall unity of the system. Similarly, we too can use the antinomies within a particular narrative to enhance the pleasure of our reading when we accept the general cohesion in the work under consideration.

The methods of nonlinear analysis acknowledge safeguards similar to those that prevent upheavals in our reading. Whatever text we take up is formed by physical boundaries as incontrovertible as any encounter in physics. For nonlinear responses, those boundaries create a sturdy defense against interpretive anarchy. The words on a printed page can evoke any number of diverse impressions, but at the same time those words put finite if multiple limits upon our impressions. Thus, no matter how ingeniously I may respond to *Pride and Prejudice*, I cannot change the fact that Elizabeth marries Darcy. Nor can I add or subtract characters in the narrative. Nor can I move the setting to Joseph Conrad's Congo River.

Finally, the process that I have been advocating can be achieved because the changes that it advances are far less radical than they might initially seem. Nonlinear thinking conforms to the associative patterns that already characterize our reading. Its inclination to move from one concept to another without obvious causal connections, its tendency to see multiplicity rather than singularity in individual observations, and its willingness to accept the unpredictability of seemingly familiar situations all reflect attitudes found in our inclinations when we read.

To be true to the process of reading, we can form impressions only from that which appears before us. Like the drop of water moving freely within the turmoil of a river, our individual progress through a work is seemingly unpredictable even as the limits of what we can do or expect remain quite clear. Imagery of the New Physics, such as that of the turbulent system, allows us to conceptualize and to discuss what in fact has been second nature to readers since the invention of the alphabet. What I propose here is not a radical departure from the status quo but rather a recognition of circumstances that have always obtained.

Appendix

The Rise of Nonlinear Science

A number of discoveries contributed to the reshaping of general assumptions about physical reality, but Einstein's work stands out as pivotal because of its wide-ranging impact upon the public's consciousness. Einstein's Special Theory of Relativity expands the features of measurements from three to four dimensions—adding duration to the familiar length, width, height—to form a space-time continuum. Within this construct the speed of light remains constant, and all other features vary according to the situation. In a devastating critique of quotidian assumptions, Einstein's Special Theory of Relativity makes the world of time and space a far more elastic place than people had previously imagined.[1]

Continuing the assault upon Cartesian assumptions, Einstein's General Theory of Relativity takes on another long-held Newtonian assumption—the effect of gravity. Einstein asserts that light curves as it moves through space, not as a result of gravitational fields but rather because space itself is a curved four-dimensional field. Matter changes the geometry of space from flat to curved in much the way a heavy object reconfigures the shape of a taut sheet on which it is resting. As a result, gravity loses its privileged position as a constant, for depending upon the conditions—traveling in a spaceship, for example—we cannot tell whether gravity or some other nonuniform motion is pulling us down.[2]

Even Einstein was awed by the apparent consequences of his work on relativity—the issue of how a person locates himself or herself when familiar reference points are destabilized—and he declined to pursue some of the more radical implications of his theories, especially at the subatomic level. However, in the 1920s the Copenhagen group, a number of scientists working in conjunction, expanded upon concepts of quanta already explored by Einstein and by Max Planck. Niels Bohr took up the assumption that Newtonian laws of physics do not apply within the configuration of the atom, and he posited a subatomic structure based on the effect of electrons' moving or remaining stable within the atomic structure. Most significantly, this work underscored the dynamics of perception, taking into account the relative, contingent features of the process. One scientist summed it up as follows: "[T]here is no deep reality for us to discover in the traditional sense, only a description of it. The reality that we observe is determined by the act of observation. It really exists when it has been measured—it is not an illusion—but there is no sense in which we can say that it exists in the absence of an act of observation."[3] In stark contrast to Newtonian science, quantum physics emerged not to resolve but rather to articulate this ambiguity.

Werner Heisenberg's Uncertainty Principle grew directly out of Bohr's work. It holds that, even in theory, both the position and the velocity of an object cannot simultaneously be measured. An observer can calculate either position or velocity as precisely as desired, but the greater the precision of one computation, the less precise the other will inevitably be. This may at first seem of interest only to nuclear physicists, since the imprecisions outlined by this principle can be discerned only at the subatomic level. In fact, indeterminacy and field theory—the related view that we and anything that we observe are located within and influenced by the same system—offer timely corrections to assumptions of certitude governing the way we see the world around us. They underscore the provisionality of Newtonian physics at microcosmic levels and facilitate thinking about interactions that occur on a plane of perception well above the subatomic range. The value of these concepts to humanists (especially those like myself with a phobia for mathematics) lies in applying their sweeping reconfiguration of the perception of the material world to analogous efforts to interpret aesthetic experiences.

New ways of thinking, which grew out of Einstein's work on relativity and the mathematical efforts of Jules-Henri Poincaré, emerged quite forcefully in mathematics and physics. They provoked a great deal of opposition within a scientific community resistant to the changes. Quantum Mechanics projected a new way of looking at material reality upon familiar concepts of the world. This approach discarded the certitude of Newtonian physics for the approximations of probability. (Of course, quantum physics does much more than that, but, in terms of how I wish to apply it to humanist thinking, the distinction made here is sufficient.)

In the mid-1920s the Austrian scientist Erwin Schrödinger, like many of his contemporaries, was struggling to come to grips with the implications of quantum physics. Schrödinger's fundamental view of science directly opposed this abandonment of the pursuit of certitude and the acceptance of mutability as an inherent feature of the world in which we exist. He made great efforts to rebut the basic assumptions of quantum physics, especially those relating to the way that perception shapes presence at the subatomic level. He particularly disputed the idea that measuring an object reconfigures its features. To show the ridiculousness of such a viewpoint, Schrödinger set up a thought problem. This is a common approach in theoretical physics in which an experiment is outlined in great detail but never actually undertaken, usually because of the physical obstacles that preclude its execution. John Gribbin explains the process in his book *In Search of Schrödinger's Cat:*

It is possible to set up an experiment in such a way that there is a precise fifty-fifty chance that one of the atoms in a lump of radioactive material will decay in a certain time and that a detector will register the decay if it does happen. [Now, quantum physicists believe that the act of measuring became a determining factor in whether the atom decayed.] Schrödinger . . . tried to show the absurdity of those implications by imagining such an experiment set in a closed room, or box, which also contains a live cat and a phial of poison, so arranged that if the radioactive decay does occur then the poison container is broken and the cat dies. In the everyday world, there is a fifty-fifty chance that the cat will be killed, and without looking inside the box we can say, quite happily, that the cat inside is either dead or alive. But now we encounter the strangeness of the quantum world. According to the theory, *neither* of the two possibilities open to the radioactive material, and therefore to the cat, has any reality unless it is observed. The atomic decay has neither happened nor not happened, the cat has neither been killed nor not killed, until we look inside the box to see what has happened. Theorists who accept the pure version of quantum mechanics say that the cat exists in some indeterminate state, neither dead nor alive, until an observer looks into the box to see how things are getting on. Nothing is real until it is observed.[4]

Schrödinger's thought experiment captured the attention of the post-Einsteinian scientific community because it freed them from a restrictive paradigm and gave them much greater flexibility in seeking an answer to the problem of complex perception. (A great irony underlies Schrödinger's demonstration. He offered it as an example of an absurd way of thinking. However, men like Niels Bohr embraced his illustration, and it has become a standard model for expressing the system of thought applied to quantum physics.)

Schrödinger's Cat and Heisenberg's Uncertainty Principle turn upon the same concept—a belief in the power of the act of apprehension to transform the fundamental features of an object. Perception stands as a subjective experience. In consequence, something has existence for me only when I observe it. This notion rejects the view of China as an objective, independent reality of one billion people located on the opposite side of the globe. Rather, it posits the concept that for each of us the country comes into existence as a subjective entity drawn from a series of impressions drawn from various media that are united by each observer into a single conception.

Analogous assumptions provide a useful foundation for examining the features of the act of reading. Until someone apprehends it, *Othello*, for instance, does not exist. Rather, what exists, in the form of a book or script, is only an artifact made up of wood pulp, printer's ink, and glue. As with China or Schrödinger's cat, an individual brings this object to life by creating a text through apprehension—the act of reading or viewing the play—and, as illustrated by Heisenberg's Uncertainty Principle, efforts to delineate and understand this text progressively reconfigure the work under consideration.

Measuring or reading defines the reality of the thing, and therefore is part of the thing itself. Like the work of Einstein and Poincaré before them, the efforts of the Copenhagen group not only resulted in important discoveries, it laid the groundwork for further insights into nonlinear perceptions: chaos or, more accurately, complexity systems that now suggest broad analytical reconfiguration, well beyond the limits of theoretical physics.

While the origins of chaos/complexity theories remain disparate, for more than one hundred years, Poincaré's studies of relativity—through an interest in topology and dynamic systems—have fueled an interest in nonlinear dynamics. Indeed, Poincaré, writing in *Science and Method* (1908), offers ideas that clearly substantiate this connection:

> A very small cause which escapes our notice determines a considerable effect that we cannot fail to see, and then we say that the effect is due to chance. If we knew exactly the laws of nature and the situation of the universe at the initial moment, we could predict exactly the situation of that same universe at a succeeding moment. But even if it were the case that the natural laws had no longer any secret for us, we could still know the situation approximately. If that enabled us to predict the succeeding situations with the same approximation, that is all we require, and we should say that the phenomenon had been predicted, that the laws govern it. But it is not always so; it may happen that small differences in the initial conditions produce very great ones in the final phenomena. A small error in the former will produce an enormous error in the latter. Prediction becomes impossible.[5]

Poincaré introduces ideas that one of the earliest proponents of complexity theory, meteorologist Edward Lorenz, would echo three-quarters of a century later. Nonetheless, until comparatively recently other scientists made little use of Poincaré's concepts, in part because they lacked the tools to make the monumental calculations necessary to pursue the implications of his ideas.

As Heinz R. Pagels notes, however, the advent of sophisticated computers has accelerated studies of nonlinearity, allowing scientists to use models requiring highly repetitive calculations, projects heretofore unthinkable. Computers can produce and evaluate amounts of data exponentially beyond the human capacity for iteration, pushing experimenters toward new ways of perceiving: "scientists have uncovered chaotic solutions hidden in nonlinear, deterministic equations, chaos that describes phenomena like the weather or the behavior of neural nets."[6] As readers have pursued the implications of nonlinear dynamics, the fundamental outlines of chaos and complexity theories have emerged in a disorienting fashion. "Non-linearity means that the act of playing the game has a way of changing the rules."[7]

"The Butterfly Effect," first described by Edward Lorenz in the 1960s, has become the most popular explanation of this phenomenon. In an effort to systematize meteorology, Lorenz found that a small disturbance, such as a mathematical error or a puff of wind, could have the cumulative impact of enforcing radical changes upon the interaction of elements within a particular system—sensitive dependence upon initial conditions. Thus, a butterfly flapping its wings in Brazil might produce thunderstorms in Texas.[8] While the enormous consequences of the butterfly's apparently random movement remain difficult to comprehend, researchers must face the more daunting challenge of determining whether such an act reflects chaotic or complex behavior—that is, is it truly random, or does some form of organization exist?

Further, complex, nonlinear systems will not yield to predictability in the same fashion that the clockwork structure of the Cartesian universe would.[9] A randomness will occur in any complex system. (That is not to say that such randomness does not exist in the Cartesian world, but rather when it does appear, observers have learned how to ignore it.) Over time the influence of this randomness will build up and create enormous change. The dynamics of the system preclude mapping this randomness, and so, as Poincaré says, "[p]rediction becomes impossible." However, the absence of the certitude that made the principles of classical physics so reassuring does not make the study of complexity pointless. Rather, in suggesting very different assumptions about perception of the physical world, related concepts like fractals and strange attractors, and other ideas from the New Physics, have presented images and eventually metaphors for a new and more sophisticated way of understanding not simply the material but the metaphysical world as well.

Notes

Chapter 1. How Do We Talk about What We Read?

1. Joyce, *A Portrait of the Artist as a Young Man*, 188.

2. For a useful summary of the evolution of this system of thought, see Demastes, *Theatre of Chaos: Beyond Absurdism, into Orderly Disorder*, 2–7. Demastes includes in this summary an illuminating account of the failure in the first century B.C. of the challenge to this system made by the philosopher Lucretius.

3. This inclination in contemporary literary interpretation to privilege definitive meaning seems strongly influenced by biblical exegesis. That practice examined the Old and New Testaments for revelations of the will of God and sought to render those revelations in language accessible to all humans. From the Enlightenment onward, readers have applied this exegetical tradition to the epistemological approach to literature: a search for meaning based upon the assumption that literature provides a means for a better understanding of the individual and of the world that he or she inhabits. This concept sees truth buried in a literary work, and the critic exhumes that truth. It reflects a conception of literature as a more palatable version of philosophy or theology, a discipline that seeks to teach us how to be better people or at the very least how to have a better sense of the world. For a detailed examination of this process, see Richard E. Palmer's *Hermeneutics: Interpretation Theory in Schleiermacher, Dilthey, Heidegger, and Gadamer.*

4. Joyce, *Ulysses*, 1.01–05.

5. Benstock, "Telemachus," 2.

6. A discussion of this process appears in James Gleick's *Chaos: Making a New Science*, 55–56.

7. Any number of books present good overviews of the critical theories of the period covered below. In particular with regard to the ideas of F. R. Leavis, Mikhail Bakhtin, and Kenneth Burke, I have benefited from the insights found in Patricia Bizzell and Bruce Herzberg, eds., *The Rhetorical Tradition: Readings from Classical Times to the Present.*

8. For a more detailed examination of Wilde's criticism, see my *Oscar Wilde and the Poetics of Ambiguity*, 17–35.

9. Leavis, *Revaluation*, 2–3.

10. Ibid., 3.

11. Bakhtin, *The Dialogic Imagination*, 262–63. Cf. also 45–49 and 312–31. The glossary expands this concept and touches on the problem of traditional approaches: "Heteroglossia is as close a conceptualization as is possible of that locus where centripetal and centrifugal forces collide; as such, it is that which a systematic linguistics must always suppress" (428).

12. Ibid., 324.

13. Frye, *Anatomy of Criticism*, 4.

14. Ibid., 6.

15. Booth, *The Rhetoric of Fiction*, 138.

16. Burke, *A Grammar of Motives*, 173.

17. Ibid., 313.

18. Barthes, *S/Z*, 105.

19. The best example of this approach remains Derrida's *Of Grammatology*. Gayatri Chakravorty Spivak's introduction and Derrida's elaboration give an excellent illustration of the process.

20. See Reed Way Dasenbrock's comments on Derrida's nostalgia for order in his essay "Taking It Personally: Reading Derrida's Responses."

21. Andrjez Gasiorek makes a similar point by juxtaposing "the linear Whig emphasis on progress [with] an equally linear postmodernist stress on decline" when he critiques Graham Swift's *Waterworld* in his *Post-War British Fiction: Realism and After*, 150.

22. Iser, *The Act of Reading*, and Jauss, *Toward an Aesthetics of Reception*.

23. For a specific critique of Iser in this regard, see my *Reading the Book of Himself: Narrative Strategies in the Works of James Joyce*, 82.

24. See Fish's *Is There a Text in This Class? The Authority of Interpretive Communities*.

25. For an interesting reflection of Fish's views of Iser, see his essay "Why No One's Afraid of Wolfgang Iser."

26. Ginzburg, *The Cheese and the Worms*.

27. Greenblatt, *Shakespearean Negotiations*.

28. For a useful examination of how Deconstruction, for example, undermines any theoretical approach that attempts to adopt it, see Mary Poovey's "Feminism and Deconstruction."

Chapter 2. Nonlinear Thinking

1. At the same time, one must acknowledge that even works like this can have pragmatic agendas. Weinberg's book, in fact, devotes a great deal of space to lobbying for the completion of the superconducting super collider that the U.S. government was building in Ellis County, Texas, a project in which he was deeply involved. (The project ultimately was canceled.)

2. At the same time, the very act of transmission brings about modifications, sometimes subtle and sometimes radical, that transform the original insights. Ideas do not reproduce like copies from a Xerox machine but rather with an organic, evolutionary bent that sophisticated thinkers accept. All words are metaphoric; scientists and humanists alike often have an imperfect and inconsistent sense of how metaphors work. N. Katherine Hayles provides a refreshing exception to this trend. See her *Chaos Bound: Orderly Disorder in Contemporary Literature and Science*. Her remarks on the relation of Gödel's theorem to metaphor are particularly useful (35).

3. John Gribbin, *In Search of Schrödinger's Cat*, 81–91, gives a useful summary of this shift in perspective.

4. For a good working distinction between linear and nonlinear, see Roger Lewin, *Complexity: Life at the Edge of Chaos*, 11.

5. In some instances this adoption involves a literalist approach, one that views chaos theory not as a metaphoric system but rather as an outline of behavior that one understands through verbatim application of the theory. Others have found that the broad scientific conceptions of the new discipline offer patterns of thought—rather than specific insights—that stimulate their own work in provocative new ways. For a more detailed critique of the work of these humanists and of the scientists who have attacked them, see my "(Meta)physics and 'the portals of discovery.'"

6. Early in *Chaos Bound* Hayles makes a useful distinction that helps one understand the harsh responses to her book and to others by literary critics working with images from nonlinear dynamics: "'chaos theory' and the 'science of chaos' are not phrases usually employed by researchers [in the hard sciences] who work in these fields. They prefer to designate their area as nonlinear dynamics, dynamical systems theory, or, more modestly yet, dynamical systems methods. To them, using 'chaos theory' or the 'science of chaos' signals that one is a dilettante rather than an expert" (8). Hayles rightly singles out the proprietary attitude of such scientists who employ such dismissive terms. Like Hayles and others working in the field, I have tried to resist what William Demastes in *Theatre of Chaos* calls "an 'objectivist's' control over their material" (8) by employing *chaos theory, complexity theory,* and *nonlinear dynamics* as interchangeable terms.

7. Hawkins, *Strange Attractors: Literature, Culture and Chaos Theory.*

8. Of course, any interdisciplinary studies raise fundamental problems. While many scientists are themselves hesitant to embrace concepts of nonlinear thinking, others are adamantly opposed to the possibility that nonscientists might do so. Although the conflict has raged over a number of areas, the fundamental objection that scientists make relates to rigor; critics assert that nonscientists do not apply the concepts of nonlinear thinking with the same precision as scientists. That may well be the case, but it is equally true that nonscientists do not apply the principles of a Newtonian worldview with the same precision. That is because the disciplines are different, and it is unfair and illogical to apply the standards of one to judge conduct in the other. In any case, these criticisms have been addressed elsewhere, and I will merely reference this exchange rather than repeat it.

9. Kuberski, *Chaosmos: Literature, Science, and Theory.*

10. Kellert, *In the Wake of Chaos*, 13.

11. Ford, *The Good Solider*, 3.

12. For a detailed explanation of wave and particle theory, especially as it relates to literature, see Demastes, *Theatre of Chaos*, 28–33.

13. Gleick, *Chaos*, 83, cites the example of cotton prices and income distribution taking the same pattern.

14. Propp, *Morphology of the Folktale.*

15. For examples of critical responses to *Finnegans Wake* that have already applied concepts of chaos and complexity theories, see Thomas Jackson Rice, *Joyce, Chaos, and Complexity*, 112–40. See also Kuberski, *Chaosmos*, 49–97.

1. Tindall, *A Reader's Guide to* Finnegans Wake; Burgess, *A Shorter* Finnegans Wake; Gordon, *Understanding* Finnegans Wake; and Rose and O'Hanlon, *Understanding* Finnegans Wake: *A Guide to the Narrative of James Joyce's Masterpiece.*

2. Arnold Goldman, in an assessment of Tindall's *Reader's Guide*, notes: "Mr. Tindall's overview lacks critical resonance, nowhere more than in assuming students will apply his techniques of linking, relating, echoing, cross-referencing, *and no others*" (emphasis in original, 106). Christopher Lehmann-Haupt critiques Anthony Burgess for "synopsizing many portions" of *Finnegans Wake* (31). Patrick McCarthy reacts to John Gordon's claim in Finnegans Wake: *A Plot Summary* to writing "a thoroughly reductive" account of Joyce's novel: "If, however, we want a definitive study of what really happens in *Finnegans Wake* . . . I suspect that we are in for a long wait" (154). J.C.C. Mays said of the Rose and O'Hanlon book: "It is curious that a book whose success rests squarely on the results of a specific contribution to *Wake* studies masquerades as a summary of the story-line for beginning-readers. Too many questions go begging which even beginning-readers want to know the answers to" (123).

3. The gist of the problem relates to Mandelbrot's proof that attempts to measure the boundary of an object like Britain lead one to a confrontation with an ever-increasing number. The more precise the measurement, the greater the length, and there is no reason to assume that this precision cannot go on toward infinite refinement and thus infinite length. From the mid- nineteenth century onward, mathematicians and physicists have struggled to understand this instability, but perceptual changes brought about by post-Einsteinian science have greatly accelerated their progress. For a useful summary of these efforts, see Gribbin, *In Search of Schrödinger's Cat*, 255–75, and Gleick, *Chaos*, 81–118.

4. Heisenberg, *Physics and Philosophy*, 79. For Heisenberg's elaboration of this view, see his chapter 5, "The Development of Philosophical Ideas since Descartes in Comparison with the New Situation in Quantum Theory," 76–92.

5. I am of course aware of an insidious Cartesian tone inherent in my own approach. I am clearly giving very specific meaning to the terms *readings, interpretations, classical science*, and *reductivist*. Further, I must admit that, to my chagrin, a measure of linearity inevitably shapes my argument. I think that this is a necessary consequence of the initial stage of the critique that I am mounting. In subsequent work, I will use the metaphors of nonlinearity—fractals, strange attractors, scaling, and so forth—to model readings that employ very different assumptions for unity.

6. Beckett et al., *Our Exagmination round His Factification for Incamination of Work in Progress.*

7. Wilson, "The Dream of H. C. Earwicker," 198.

8. Levin, *James Joyce*, 140.

9. Tindall, *A Reader's Guide to James Joyce*, 237.

10. Hart, *Structure and Motif in* Finnegans Wake, 14.

11. Benstock, *Joyce-agains Wake*, 42.

12. Cheng, *Shakespeare and Joyce*, 1–2.

13. Hayman, *The Wake in Transit*, 2.

14. Norris, *Joyce's Web*, 139.

15. In fairness to David Hayman, Danis Rose, John O'Hanlan and other genetic scholars, an entire area of *Wake* studies has devoted itself to a broad understanding of the work. Up to now, however, these practitioners have succeeded only in producing complex interpretations based upon complex principles, and by their own admission have not yet arrived at a final solution.

16. Rice, "The Complexity of *Finnegans Wake*." See also Mackey, *Chaos Theory and James Joyce's Everyman*.

17. Joyce, *Finnegans Wake*. All references are to this edition and cite page and line number.

18. Joyce, *Letters of James Joyce*, III.79.

19. See, for example, Burgess, *ReJoyce*, 260; Adaline Glasheen, "The Opening Paragraphs (Contd.)"; Barbara DiBernard, *Alchemy and* Finnegans Wake, 87–88, 91, and 100–107; and Beryl Schlossman, *Joyce's Catholic Comedy of Language*, 43, 72, 77, 93, 145, 151, 153, and 178–80. David Hayman glancingly touches upon "the trinitarian truth" of the passage. However, he fails to exploit its possibilities, dismissing it as "tongue-in-cheek" and focusing instead on biographical material (*The* Wake *in Transit*, 33, 102).

20. O'Dwyer, "Czarnowski and *Finnegans Wake*." One finds a similar archetypal treatment of St. Patrick in Timothy Martin's *Joyce and Wagner: A Study of Influence*, 76, 91, 100, 118, 127, and 135.

21. See Joyce's *Letters*, III.140 and I.241.

22. O'Dwyer, "Czarnowski and *Finnegans Wake*," 281.

23. Boyle, *James Joyce's Pauline Vision*, 45ff.

24. This approach does not, of course, suggest that one needs to be a practicing Catholic to comprehend Joyce, but it does assert that knowledge of Joyce's religious identity enhances one's appreciation of his writings.

25. See Jack Cohen and Ian Stewart, *The Collapse of Chaos: Discovering Simplicity in a Complex World*, 11 and 377–90. A more detailed and esoteric articulation of this concept appears in James Lovelock's *The Ages of Gaia*.

26. See, for example, Burgess, *ReJoyce*, 233; Joseph Campbell and Henry Morton Robinson, *A Skeleton Key to* Finnegans Wake, 40–42; and Roland McHugh, *Annotations to* Finnegans Wake, 8–10.

27. De Certeau, in *The Writing of History*, neatly sums up the paradigm shift that he perceives the discipline undergoing:

> Forty years ago a first critique of "scientism" revealed the relation of "objective" history to a place, that of the subject. In analyzing what Raymond Aron has termed a "dissolution of the object," this critique took from history the privilege in which the discipline had taken so much pride when it claimed to reconstitute the "truth" of events. Moreover, "objective" history upheld with this idea of truth a model derived from a former philosophy, or from a theology dating from an even earlier time. It limited itself to translating truth in terms of historical "facts"—and the happy days of this positivism are over. (58)

28. Graham, Sullivan, and Richter, "'Mind Your Hats Goan In!': Notes on the Museyroom Episode of *Finnegans Wake*." For evidence of the continuing inclination to read along these lines, see Cheng, "The General and the Sepoy: Imperialism and Power in the Museyroom," 258–68. Although Cheng's essay takes a narrower

focus than the Graham, Sullivan, and Richter piece, it operates from the same epistemological assumptions.

29. Rose and O'Hanlon, *Understanding* Finnegans Wake, 10.

30. For a detailed summary of Lorenz's work, see Gleick, *Chaos*, 9–33.

31. Gleick, *Chaos*, 48.

Chapter 4. "And they lived happily ever after"

1. In the cherry tree episode, George Washington, acting on impulse, chops down the cherry tree and then refuses to lie to escape punishment. The Spartan boy steals a fox and, when caught with the animal hidden under his cloak, stoically endures the fox's ultimately fatal bites rather than reveal its presence. Each story celebrates the nobility of the young man featured in its narrative, but each foregrounds a very different moral worldview sharply at odds with the other. A reader may accept or resist the conventional interpretation that each tale invites, but one cannot ignore that invitation in the creation of meaning for the story.

2. One finds a good summary of this shift from the loosely configured oral tales to the more formal written stories in Jack Zipes, *Breaking the Magic Spell: Radical Theories of Folk and Fairy Tales*, 5–9.

3. For a survey of criticism of fairy tales from Plato to contemporary critics, see Peter Gilet, *Vladimir Propp and the Universal Folktale: Recommissioning an Old Paradigm—Story as Initiation*, 13–48. Gilet's writing is plodding and at times unintelligible, but he does manage to pull together useful information for one seeking to understand the critical tradition for the study of the fairy tale.

4. Zipes, *Breaking the Magic Spell*, 12.

5. Tatar, *Off with Their Heads!* xv.

6. One finds a good overview of these two approaches in Alan Dundes' introduction to the second edition of Propp's *Morphology of the Folktale*, xi–xiii.

7. Bettelheim, *The Uses of Enchantment: The Meaning and Importance of Fairy Tales*.

8. See, for example, Joyce Thomas, *Inside the Wolf's Body: Concepts of the Fairy Tale*; Marina Warner, *From the Beast to the Blond: On Fairy Tales and Their Tellers*; and continuing works by Zipes, most recently, *Happily Ever After: Fairy Tales, Children, and the Culture Industry*.

9. Zipes, *Breaking the Magic Spell*, and Bettelheim, *The Uses of Enchantment*, both rest their arguments on these assumptions.

10. Zipes, *Breaking the Magic Spell*, 97. He continues this critique, updating the transgressions of "the culture industry," in his 1997 book, *Happily Ever After*.

11. Even the frame of each tale has a prescriptive familiarity that seems never to vary. Tell a room full of people that you are going to begin a story with "once upon a time," and they know that you will end with "and they lived happily ever after."

12. There are few examples of traditional, scholarly readings of *Harry Potter and the Sorcerer's Stone*. However, for a thorough, if extremely conventional, assessment of the framework of the Harry Potter series, see Nicholas Tucker, "The Rise and Rise of Harry Potter." Although Tucker does not label Rowling's works as fairy tales, he does compare them to the Cinderella story. Tucker critiques the series for being too

distant from the experiences of contemporary children, but that, of course, describes a feature central to any fairy tale.

13. As Tatar notes in *Off with Their Heads!* 224, a disruption in the normal family structure, such as a stepmother's replacing a mother, can undermine the way the unit functions. This disruption can, temporarily at least, cause the good father to do a bad thing, like abandoning his children in the woods. When the stepmother dies, the father's ability to act according to the goodness in his nature returns.

14. Lévi-Strauss, *The Cooked and the Raw,* 5.

Chapter 5. "I sing of arms and of a man"

1. Tolkien, "*Beowulf:* The Monsters and the Critics," 246.

2. For a good overview of this process, see John D. Niles, "*Beowulf* in Literary History."

3. See, for example, W. W. Lawrence, Beowulf *and the Epic Tradition.*

4. In delineating these characteristics, I have drawn on the definition of *epic* provided by C. Hugh Holman in *A Handbook to Literature,* 194. While other definitions exist, they generally highlight the same features. Tolkien himself rejected the term *epic* in favor of *elegy* ("*Beowulf:* The Monsters and the Critics," 246). However, the preponderance of evidence argues that, if any term must be applied to *Beowulf, epic* most suits its characterizing features.

5. All quotations from the poem come from the Seamus Heaney translation, *Beowulf.* Line numbers identify passages.

6. See, for example, Harry Berger Jr. and M. Marshall Leicester, "Social Structure as Doom: The Limits of Heroism in *Beowulf*"; John D. Niles, "*Beowulf* in Literary History"; John M. Hill, *The Cultural World in* Beowulf; and James W. Earl, "*Beowulf* and the Origins of Civilization."

7. Thormann, "*Beowulf* and the Enjoyment of Violence."

8. Ibid., 67–68.

9. For recent examples, see Mark Amodio, "Affective Criticism, Oral Poetics, and Beowulf's Fight with the Dragon"; Clive Tolley, "*Beowulf's* Scyld Scefing Episode: Some Norse and Finnish Analogues"; and John D. Niles, "Understanding *Beowulf:* Oral Poetry Acts."

10. In another context, Northrop Frye reminds us that an oral culture, which *Beowulf* at the very least imitates, keeps the past in the present by the continual repetition of the details of specific events, a repetition essential to the preservation of knowledge of those events. See Frye, *The Great Code: The Bible and Literature,* 22.

Chapter 6. "A time for every purpose under heaven"

1. In examining the Book of Job, I have focused on a portion of the Bible accepted by all faiths that use the Bible as a theological reference. When making allusions to the Bible as a whole, I generally have the King James version in mind, the version most often read as literature and, since its appearance, the version of choice for literary allusions to the Bible.

2. Frye, *The Great Code,* 42.

3. For a detailed examination of this process, see Palmer, *Hermeneutics.*

4. Beckett, *Waiting for Godot*, 9a–9b.

5. Although the two terms may seem to raise their own formidable problems of interpretation, James Joyce in the opening chapter of *Ulysses* deftly distinguishes between the two:

—You're not a believer, are you? Haines asked. I mean, a believer in the narrow sense of the word. Creation from nothing and miracles and a personal God.

—There's only one sense of the word it seems to me, Stephen said. (*U*, 1:611–14)

6. MacLeish, *J.B.: A Play in Verse*. Other instances abound in literature and folktales. Robert Frost's poem "The Masque of Reason" provides an alternate point of view.

7. While I am wholeheartedly advocating an alternative literary reading of the Book of Job, I do not mean to dismiss traditional hermeneutic approaches to theological interpretations. One finds an excellent example of the rich comprehension that grows out of careful linear reading in the explication of the story of David and Bathsheba offered in Meir Sternberg's examination of the literary aspects of the Bible, *The Poetics of Biblical Narrative: Ideological Literature and the Drama of Reading*. Sternberg's interpretation gives a wonderful account of the diverse elements of the story of infidelity, murder, and abuse of power. At the same time, it shows how much dexterity is required to resolve apparent contradictions even in this relatively straightforward account. In the end the success of Sternberg's reading hinges on the reader's acceptance of a number of assumptions that may or may not be justified but are crucial in resolving the ambiguities inherent in the narrative.

8. Sternberg, *The Poetics of Biblical Narrative*, 345–46.

9. Ibid., 346.

10. Three such efforts appear in a collection of essays relating to feminist approaches to portions of the Bible: Lillian R. Klein, "Job and the Womb: Text about Men, Subtext about Women"; Ellen van Wolde, "The Development of Job: Mrs. Job as Catalyst"; and Lyn M. Bechtel, "A Feminist Approach to the Book of Job." Bechtel's views offer the most detailed and unconventional approach, and they will be examined here in some detail.

11. Bechtel, "A Feminist Approach to the Book of Job," 224.

12. Ibid., 225.

13. Ibid., 252.

Chapter 7. Oscar Wilde and the Fabrication of an Irish Identity

1. See, for example, Cornel West, *Race Matters*.

2. The work of Edward Said served as the catalyst for this interest. Most particularly, *Orientalism* set up a paradigm for subsequent critics to follow. Subsequent studies by Homi Bhabha have also spurred others to pursue these issues. See his *The Location of Culture*.

3. The best-known and most influential broad studies have been David Lloyd, *Anomalous States: Irish Writing and the Post-Colonial Movement*, and Declan Kiberd, *Inventing Ireland: The Literature of the Modern Nation*. Numerous Joyceans have taken up this concern. They include Vincent Cheng, *Joyce, Race, and Empire*; Enda Duffy, *The Subaltern Ulysses*; and Emer Nolan, *James Joyce and Nationalism*.

For the best explanation of postcolonial/post-colonial distinctions, see Lance Pettitt's *Screening Ireland*.

4. Kuch, "Kiberd on Ireland's Colonial Conundrums," 18.

5. Joyce, *A Portrait of the Artist as a Young Man*, 252–53.

6. For examples of these approaches, see Kerry Powell, *Oscar Wilde and the Theatre of the 1890s*; Peter Raby, The Importance of Being Earnest: *A Reader's Companion*; and Sos Eltis, *Revising Wilde: Society and Subversion in the Plays of Oscar Wilde*.

7. Wilde, *The Writings of Oscar Wilde*, 526. Future references will be to this edition and will be cited parenthetically.

8. Maggie Smith's powerful rendering of the character in the West End in 1993 exemplified this quite well, though it did not rely upon an Irish characterization. Rather, Smith's interpretation underscored a particular approach to Englishness, a class-conscious, exclusionary attitude that gives a petty and claustrophobic aura to English identity. Nonetheless, her Lady Bracknell emerged as a different character and Wilde's drama a different play because of this approach.

Chapter 8. What Is to Be Done?

1. Dasenbrock, "Taking It Personally: Reading Derrida's Responses."

Appendix. The Rise of Nonlinear Science

1. For a detailed explanation of Einstein's special theory of relativity, see Gribbin, *In Search of Schrödinger's Cat*, 43.

2. For an excellent explanation of this theory, paraphrasing Einstein's epiphanic moment in imagining his theory, see Rice, *Joyce, Chaos, and Complexity*, 148. Rice sums up the process through the following example: "first, drop a rock off a cliff and observe how it speeds away from you, standing there at apparent rest (nonuniform motion); second, jump from the cliff just as you drop the rock and observe how both you and the rock seem to be at rest, or in constant uniform motion; you have no sensation of gravity."

3. John D. Barrow, quoted in Rice, *Joyce, Chaos, and Complexity*, 151–52.

4. Gribbin, *In Search of Schrödinger's Cat*, 2–3.

5. Poincaré, *Science and Method*, 67–68.

6. Pagels, *The Dreams of Reason*, 49.

7. Gleick, *Chaos*, 24.

8. Lorenz, "Deterministic Nonperiodic Flow," 130–41.

9. Pagels, *The Dreams of Reason*, 74–76.

Bibliography

Amodio, Mark. "Affective Criticism, Oral Poetics, and Beowulf's Fight with the Dragon." *Oral Tradition* 10 (March 1995): 54–90.

Bakhtin, Mikhail M. *The Dialogic Imagination: Four Essays.* Ed. Michael Holquist. Trans. Caryl Emerson and Michael Holquist. Austin: University of Texas Press, 1981.

Barthes, Roland. *The Pleasure of the Text.* New York: Hill and Wang, 1974.

———. *S/Z.* Trans. Richard Miller. New York: Noonday Press, 1974.

Bechtel, Lyn M. "A Feminist Approach to the Book of Job." In *A Companion to Wisdom Literature,* ed. Athalya Brenner, 222–51. Sheffield, U.K.: Sheffield Academic Press, 1995.

Beckett, Samuel, et al. *Our Exagmination round His Factification for Incamination of Work in Progress.* 1929. Reprint, New York: New Directions, 1962.

———. *Waiting for Godot.* New York: Grove Press, 1954.

Benstock, Bernard. *Joyce-agains Wake: An Analysis of* Finnegans Wake. Seattle and London: University of Washington Press, 1965.

———. "Telemachus." In *James Joyce's* Ulysses: *Critical Essays,* ed. Clive Hart and David Hayman, 1–16. Berkeley and Los Angeles: University of California Press, 1974.

Berger, Harry, Jr., and M. Marshall Leicester. "Social Structure as Doom: The Limits of Heroism in *Beowulf.*" In *Old English Studies in Honor of John C. Pope,* edited by Robert B. Burlin and Edward B. Irving, Jr., 37–79. Toronto: University of Toronto Press, 1974.

Bettelheim, Bruno. *The Uses of Enchantment: The Meaning and Importance of Fairy Tales.* New York: Knopf, 1977.

Bhabha, Homi K. *The Location of Culture.* London: Routledge, 1994.

Bizzell, Patricia, and Bruce Herzberg, eds. *The Rhetorical Tradition: Readings from Classical Times to the Present.* Boston: Bedford Books of St. Martin's Press, 1990.

Booth, Wayne. *The Company We Keep: An Ethics of Fiction.* Berkeley: University of California Press, 1988.

———. *The Rhetoric of Fiction.* Chicago: University of Chicago Press, 1961.

Boyle, Robert. *James Joyce's Pauline Vision: A Catholic Exposition.* Carbondale and Edwardsville: Southern Illinois University Press, 1978.

Burgess, Anthony. *ReJoyce.* New York: Norton, 1965.

———. *A Shorter* Finnegans Wake. London: Faber and Faber, 1966.

Burke, Kenneth. *A Grammar of Motives.* Berkeley and Los Angeles: University of California Press, 1969.

Campbell, Joseph, and Henry Morton Robinson. *A Skeleton Key to* Finnegans Wake. 1944. Reprint, New York: Viking, 1972.

Cheng, Vincent. "The General and the Sepoy: Imperialism and Power in the

Museyroom." In *Critical Essays on James Joyce's* Finnegans Wake, ed. Patrick A. McCarthy, 258–68. New York: G. K. Hall, 1992.

———. *Joyce, Race, and Empire*. Cambridge: Cambridge University Press, 1995.

———. *Shakespeare and Joyce: A Study of* Finnegans Wake. University Park and London: Pennsylvania State University Press, 1984.

Cohen, Jack, and Ian Stewart. *The Collapse of Chaos: Discovering Simplicity in a Complex World*. New York: Viking, 1994.

Dasenbrock, Reed Way. "Taking It Personally: Reading Derrida's Responses." *College English* 56 (1994): 261–79.

de Certeau, Michel. *The Writing of History*. Trans. Tom Conley. New York: Columbia University Press, 1988.

Demastes, William W. *Theatre of Chaos: Beyond Absurdism, into Orderly Disorder*. Cambridge: Cambridge University Press, 1998.

Derrida, Jacques. *Of Grammatology*. Trans. Gayatri Chakravorty Spivak. Baltimore and London: Johns Hopkins University Press, 1974.

de Saussure, Ferdinand. *Course in General Linguistics*. Ed. Charles Bally and Albert Sechehaye. Trans. Wade Bashen. New York: Philosophical Library, 1959.

DiBernard, Barbara. *Alchemy and* Finnegans Wake. Albany: State University of New York Press, 1980.

Duffy, Enda. *The Subaltern* Ulysses. Minneapolis: University of Minnesota Press, 1994.

Earl, James W. "*Beowulf* and the Origins of Civilization." In *Speaking Two Languages: Traditional Disciplines and Contemporary Theory in Medieval Studies*, ed. Allen J. Frantzen, 65–89. Albany: State University of New York Press, 1991.

Eltis, Sos. *Revising Wilde: Society and Subversion in the Plays of Oscar Wilde*. Oxford: Clarendon Press, 1996.

Fish, Stanley. *Is There a Text in This Class? The Authority of Interpretive Communities*. Cambridge: Harvard University Press, 1980.

———. "Why No One's Afraid of Wolfgang Iser." *Diacritics* 11 (Spring 1981): 2–13.

Ford, Ford Madox. *The Good Soldier: A Tale of Passion*. New York: Vintage, 1968.

Frye, Northrop. *Anatomy of Criticism: Four Essays*. Princeton: Princeton University Press, 1957.

———. *The Great Code: The Bible and Literature*. New York and London: Harcourt Brace Jovanovich, 1982.

Gardner, John. *Grendel*. New York: Knopf, 1971.

Gasiorek, Andrjez. *Post-War British Fiction: Realism and After*. London and New York: E. Arnold, 1995.

Gilet, Peter. *Vladimir Propp and the Universal Folktale: Recommissioning an Old Paradigm—Story as Initiation*. New York: Peter Lang, 1998.

Gillespie, Michael Patrick. "(Meta)physics and 'the portals of discovery'." *James Joyce Quarterly* 34 (1997): 597–612.

———. *Oscar Wilde and the Poetics of Ambiguity*. Gainesville: University Press of Florida, 1996.

———. *Reading the Book of Himself: Narrative Strategies in the Works of James Joyce*. Columbus: Ohio State University Press, 1989.

Ginzburg, Carlo. *The Cheese and the Worms: The Cosmos of a Sixteenth-Century*

Miller. Trans. John and Anne Tedeschi. Baltimore: Johns Hopkins University Press, 1980.

Glasheen, Adaline. "The Opening Paragraphs (Contd.)." *A Wake Newslitter* 2 (1965): 17–22.

Gleick, James. *Chaos: Making a New Science.* New York: Penguin, 1988.

Goldman, Arnold. Review of *A Reader's Guide to James Joyce*, by William York Tindall. *Review of English Studies* 22 (1971): 103–6.

Gordon, John. Finnegans Wake: *A Plot Summary.* Syracuse: Syracuse University Press, 1986.

Graham, Philip Lamar, Philip B. Sullivan, and G. F. Richter. "'Mind Your Hats Goan In!': Notes on the Museyroom Episode of *Finnegans Wake.*" *The Analyst* 21 and 22 (July and October 1962): 1–21; 1–24.

Greenblatt, Stephen. *Shakespearean Negotiations: The Circulation of Social Energy in Renaissance England.* Berkeley and Los Angeles: University of California Press, 1988.

Gribbin, John. *In Search of Schrödinger's Cat: Quantum Physics and Reality.* New York: Bantam Books, 1984.

Hart, Clive. *Structure and Motif in* Finnegans Wake. Evanston, Ill.: Northwestern University Press, 1962.

Hawkins, Harriett. *Strange Attractors: Literature, Culture and Chaos Theory.* New York: Prentice Hall, 1995.

Hayles, N. Katherine. *Chaos Bound: Orderly Disorder in Contemporary Literature and Science.* Ithaca and London: Cornell University Press, 1990.

Hayman, David. *The Wake in Transit.* Ithaca: Cornell University Press, 1990.

Heaney, Seamus, trans. *Beowulf.* New York: Farrar, Straus, and Giroux, 2000.

Heisenberg, Werner. *Physics and Philosophy: The Revolution in Modern Science.* New York: Harper, 1958.

Herring, Philip. *Joyce's Uncertainty Principle.* Princeton: Princeton University Press, 1987.

Hill, John M. *The Cultural World in* Beowulf. Toronto: University of Toronto Press, 1995.

Holman, C. Hugh. *A Handbook to Literature.* 3rd ed. Indianapolis: Odyssey Press, 1972.

Iser, Wolfgang. *The Act of Reading: A Theory of Aesthetic Response.* Baltimore and London: Johns Hopkins University Press, 1978.

Jauss, Hans Robert. *Toward an Aesthetics of Reception.* Minneapolis: University of Minnesota Press, 1982.

Joyce, James. *Finnegans Wake.* New York: Viking, 1939.

———. *Letters of James Joyce.* Vol. ed. Stuart Gilbert. New York: Viking Press, 1957; reissued with corrections 1966. Vols. II and III ed. Ed. Richard Ellmann. New York: Viking, 1966.

———. *A Portrait of the Artist as a Young Man.* Ed. Chester Anderson. New York: Viking, 1964.

———. *Ulysses.* Ed. Hans Walter Gabler. New York: Random House, 1986.

Kellert, Stephen H. *In the Wake of Chaos: Unpredictable Order in Dynamical Systems.* Chicago and London: University of Chicago Press, 1993.

Kiberd, Declan. *Inventing Ireland: The Literature of the Modern Nation*. Cambridge: Harvard University Press, 1995.

Klein, Lillian R. "Job and the Womb: Text about Men, Subtext about Women." In *A Companion to Wisdom Literature*, edited by Athalya Brenner, 186–200. Sheffield, U.K.: Sheffield Academic Press, 1995.

Kuberski, Philip. *Chaosmos: Literature, Science, and Theory*. Albany: State University of New York Press, 1994.

Kuch, Peter. "Kiberd on Ireland's Colonial Conundrums." *James Joyce Literary Supplement* 11 (1997): 18.

Lawrence, W. W. *Beowulf and the Epic Tradition*. New York: Hafner, 1967.

Leavis, F. R. *Revaluation: Tradition and Development in English Poetry*. London: Chatto and Windus, 1936.

Lehmann-Haupt, Christopher. Review of *A Shorter Finnegans Wake*, by Anthony Burgess. *New York Times*, March 15, 1969, 31.

Levin, Harry. *James Joyce: A Critical Introduction*. 1941. Rev. and augmented ed. Norfolk, Conn.: New Directions, 1960.

Lévi-Strauss, Claude. *The Cooked and the Raw: Introduction to a Science of Mythology*. Vol. 1. Trans. John and Doreen Weightman. New York and Evanston: Harper and Row, 1969.

Lewin, Roger. *Complexity: Life at the Edge of Chaos*. New York: Macmillan, 1992.

Lloyd, David. *Anomalous States: Irish Writing and the Post-Colonial Movement*. Dublin: Lilliput Press, 1993.

Longino, Helen E. *Science as Social Knowledge: Values and Objectivity in Scientific Inquiry*. Princeton: Princeton University Press, 1990.

Lorenz, Edward. "Deterministic Nonperiodic Flow." *Journal of the Atmospheric Sciences* 20 (1963): 130–41.

Lovelock, James. *The Ages of Gaia*. New York: Norton, 1988.

Mackey, Peter Francis. *Chaos Theory and James Joyce's Everyman*. Gainesville: University Press of Florida, 1999.

MacLeish, Archibald. *J.B.: A Play in Verse*. Boston: Houghton Mifflin, 1958.

Magalaner, Marvin. *Time of Apprenticeship: The Fiction of Young James Joyce*. London: Abelard-Schuman, 1959.

Martin, Timothy. *Joyce and Wagner: A Study of Influence*. Cambridge: Cambridge University Press, 1991.

Mays, J.C.C. Review of *Understanding Finnegans Wake*, by Danis Rose and John O'Hanlon. *Irish University Review* 13 (1983): 123–24.

McCarthy, Patrick. Review of *Finnegans Wake: A Plot Summary*, by John Gordon. *James Joyce Quarterly* 25 (1987): 154–56.

McCormack, Jerusha. *Wilde the Irishman*. New Haven and London: Yale University Press, 1995.

McHugh, Roland. *Annotations to Finnegans Wake*. Rev. ed. Baltimore and London: Johns Hopkins University Press, 1991.

Niles, John D. "*Beowulf* in Literary History." *Exemplaria* 5 (1993): 79–110.

———. "Understanding *Beowulf*: Oral Poetry Acts." *Journal of American Folklore* 106 (1993): 131–55.

Nolan, Emer. *James Joyce and Nationalism*. London: Routledge, 1995.

Noon, William, S.J. *Joyce and Aquinas.* New Haven: Yale University Press, 1957.

Norris, Margot. *The De-Centered Universe of* Finnegans Wake: *A Structuralist Analysis.* Baltimore: Johns Hopkins University Press, 1974.

———. *Joyce's Web: The Social Unraveling of Modernism.* Austin: University of Texas Press, 1992.

O'Dwyer, Riana. "Czarnowski and *Finnegans Wake:* A Study of the Cult of the Hero." *James Joyce Quarterly* 17 (1980): 281–91.

Pagels, Heinz R. *The Dreams of Reason: The Computer and the Rise of the Sciences of Complexity.* New York: Simon and Schuster, 1988.

Palmer, Richard E. *Hermeneutics: Interpretation Theory in Schleiermacher, Dilthey, Heidegger, and Gadamer.* Evanston, Ill.: Northwestern University Press, 1969.

Pettitt, Lance. *Screening Ireland.* New York: St. Martin's Press, 2000.

Poincaré, Jules-Henri. *Science and Method* (1908). Trans. Francis Maitland. New York: Dover Publications, 1952.

Poovey, Mary. "Feminism and Deconstruction." *Feminist Studies* 14 (1988): 51–65.

Powell, Kerry. *Oscar Wilde and the Theatre of the 1890s.* Cambridge: Cambridge University Press, 1990.

Propp, Vladimir. *Morphology of the Folktale.* 2d ed. Trans. Laurence Scott. Intro. Alan Dundes. Austin and London: University of Texas Press, 1968.

Raby, Peter. The Importance of Being Earnest: *A Reader's Companion.* New York: Twayne, 1995.

Rice, Thomas Jackson. "The Complexity of *Finnegans Wake.*" In *Joyce Studies Annual,* 79–98. Austin: University of Texas Press, 1995.

———. *Joyce, Chaos, and Complexity.* Urbana and Chicago: University of Illinois Press, 1997.

Rose, Danis, and John O'Hanlon. *Understanding* Finnegans Wake: *A Guide to the Narrative of James Joyce's Masterpiece.* New York and London: Garland, 1982.

Russo, John Paul. *I. A. Richards: His Life and Work.* Baltimore: Johns Hopkins University Press, 1995.

Said, Edward. *Orientalism.* New York: Pantheon, 1978.

Schlossman, Beryl. *Joyce's Catholic Comedy of Language.* Madison: University of Wisconsin Press, 1985.

Sternberg, Meir. *The Poetics of Biblical Narrative: Ideological Literature and the Drama of Reading.* Bloomington: Indiana University Press, 1985.

Stoppard, Tom. *Arcadia.* London: Faber and Faber, 1993.

Sullivan, Kevin. *Joyce among the Jesuits.* New York: Columbia University Press, 1958.

Tatar, Maria. *Off with Their Heads! Fairy Tales and the Culture of Childhood.* Princeton: Princeton University Press, 1992.

Thomas, Joyce. *Inside the Wolf's Body: Concepts of the Fairy Tale.* Sheffield, U.K.: Sheffield Academic Press, 1989.

Thormann, Janet. "*Beowulf* and the Enjoyment of Violence." *Literature and Psychology* 33.1 and 2 (1997): 65–76.

Tindall, William York. *A Reader's Guide to* Finnegans Wake. New York: Farrar, Straus, Giroux, 1969.

———. *A Reader's Guide to James Joyce.* New York: Noonday Press, 1959.

Tolkien, J.R.R. "*Beowulf*: The Monsters and the Critics." *Proceedings of the British Academy* 22 (1936): 245–95.

Tolley, Clive. "*Beowulf*'s Scyld Scefing Episode: Some Norse and Finnish Analogues." *Nordic Yearbook of Folklore* 52 (1996): 7–48.

Tucker, Nicholas. "The Rise and Rise of Harry Potter." *Children's Literature in Education* 30 (1999): 221–34.

van Wolde, Ellen. "The Development of Job: Mrs. Job as Catalyst." In *A Companion to Wisdom Literature*, ed. Athalya Brenner, 201–20. Sheffield, U.K.: Sheffield Academic Press, 1995.

Warner, Marina. *From the Beast to the Blond: On Fairy Tales and Their Tellers*. London: Chatto and Windus, 1994.

West, Cornel. *Race Matters*. Boston: Beacon Press, 1993.

Weinberg, Steven. *Dreams of a Final Theory*. New York: Pantheon, 1992.

Wilde, Oscar. *The Picture of Dorian Gray*. Ed. Isobel Murray. London: Oxford University Press, 1974.

———. *The Writings of Oscar Wilde*. Oxford and New York: Oxford University Press, 1989.

Wilson, Edmund. "The Dream of H. C. Earwicker." In *The Triple Thinkers and The Wound and the Bow: A Combined Volume*. Boston: Northeastern University Press, 1984.

Wimsatt, W. K., Jr., and Monroe Beardsley. "The Intentional Fallacy." *The Sewanee Review* 54 (1946): 3–23.

Wolf, Tom. *Bonfire of the Vanities*. New York: Farrar, Straus, Giroux, 1987.

Zipes, Jack. *Breaking the Magic Spell: Radical Theories of Folk and Fairy Tales*. Austin: University of Texas Press, 1979.

———. *Happily Ever After: Fairy Tales, Children, and the Culture Industry*. New York and London: Routledge, 1997.

Index

Michael Patrick Gillespie is the Louise Edna Goeden Professor of English at Marquette University. He has written several books on the works of James Joyce and Oscar Wilde. He recently published a study of the canon of William Kennedy and edited a collection of essays on nonlinear views of Joyce's writing.